AROUND chicago WITH KIDS

2nd Edition

by Nancy Maes

Fodor's Travel Publications
New York • Toronto • London • Sydney • Auckland

www.fodors.com

CREDITS
Writer: Nancy Maes

Series Editors: Karen Cure, Andrea Lehman
Editor: Andrea Lehman
Editorial Production: Ira-Neil Dittersdorf
Production/Manufacturing: Yexenia Markland

Design: Fabrizio La Rocca, *creative director;*
Tigist Getachew, *art director*
Illustration and Series Design: Rico Lins, Keren Ora
Admoni/Rico Lins Studio

ABOUT THE WRITER
Nancy Maes, author of the *Chicago Tribune*'s "Family Fare" column, is also the mother of two sons. She received the Award for Outstanding Contribution to Children's Theatre in 1998 from the Illinois Theatre Association and is a member of the Advisory Board of the Chicago Children's Humanities Festival.

FODOR'S AROUND CHICAGO WITH KIDS

Copyright © 2002 by Fodors LLC

ISBN 0-679-00913-2
ISSN 1526-1379
Second Edition

IMPORTANT TIPS
Although all prices, opening times, and other details in this book are based on information supplied to us at press time, changes occur all the time in the travel world, and Fodor's cannot accept responsibility for facts that become outdated or for inadvertent errors or omissions. So always confirm information when it matters, especially if you're making a detour to visit a specific place.

SPECIAL SALES
Fodor's Travel Publications are available at special discounts for bulk purchases for sales promotions or premiums. Special editions, including personalized covers, excerpts of existing guides, and corporate imprints, can be created in large quantities for special needs. For more information, contact your local bookseller or Special Markets, Fodor's Travel Publications, 280 Park Avenue, New York, NY 10017. Inquiries from Canada should be directed to your local Canadian bookseller or sent to Random House of Canada, Ltd., Marketing Dept., 2775 Matheson Boulevard East, Mississauga, Ontario L4W 4P7. Inquiries from the United Kingdom should be sent to Fodor's Travel Publications, 20 Vauxhall Bridge Road, London, England SW1V 2SA.

PRINTED IN THE UNITED STATES OF AMERICA
10 9 8 7 6 5 4 3 2 1

COUNTDOWN TO GOOD TIMES

Get Ready, Get Set!

68 Adler Planetarium and Astronomy Museum

67 American Girl Place

66 Art Institute of Chicago

65 Bronzeville Children's Museum

64 Brookfield Zoo

63 Buccaneer Pirate Adventure Cruises

62 Caldwell Woods

61 Chicago Botanic Garden

60 Chicago Children's Museum

59 Chicago Cultural Center

58 Chicago Historical Society

57 Chicago Mercantile Exchange

56 Chicago Music Mart at DePaul Center

55 Chicago Playworks

54 Chicago White Sox

53 Diversey Miniature Golf

52 DuPage Children's Museum

51 DuSable Museum of African American History

50 Eli's Cheesecake World

49 Emerald City Theatre Company

48 ESPN Zone

47 Field Museum of Natural History

46 Frank Lloyd Wright Home and Studio

45 Garfield Park Conservatory

44 Grosse Point Lighthouse

43 The Grove

42 Hancock Observatory

41 Harold Washington Playlot Park

40 Health World

39 Illinois Railway Museum

38 Indian Boundary Park

37 International Museum of Surgical Science

36 John G. Shedd Aquarium

35 Kohl Children's Museum

34 The L

33 Lakefront Bike Way

32 Lattof YMCA

31 Let's Dress Up

30 Lifeline Theatre KidSeries

29 Lincoln Park Zoo

28 Mexican Fine Arts Center Museum

27 Millennium Park

26 Mitchell Museum of the American Indian

25 Museum of Broadcast Communications

24 Museum of Contemporary Art

23 Museum of Holography

22 Museum of Science and Industry

21 Navy Pier

20 New Maxwell Street Market

19 North Avenue Beach

18 North Branch Bicycle Trail

17 North Park Village Nature Center

16 Oriental Institute Museum

15 Peace Museum

14 Pedway

13 Peggy Notebaert Nature Museum

12 Rainbow Falls Water Park

11 Rosenbaum ARTiFACT Center

10 Ryerson Woods

9 Sculpture Alfresco Walking Tour

8 Sears Tower Skydeck

7 Six Flags Great America

6 Skokie Northshore Sculpture Park

5 Sports Park

4 Spring Valley Nature Center and Volkening Heritage Farm

3 Swedish American Museum Center

2 Terra Museum of American Art

1 Thomas Hughes Children's Library

Extra! Extra!

High Fives

Something for Everyone

All Around Town

Many Thanks!

GET READY, GET SET!

C hicago's motto, *"urbs en horto,"* means "city in a garden." And it is indeed a lush garden for those who are growing themselves. This midwestern metropolis is ripe with world-class cultural institutions that are innovative and child friendly. Take, for example, the Museum of Science and Industry, one of the first U.S. museums with hands-on activities. The Art Institute of Chicago was the nation's first art museum to design exhibits just for kids, and Chicago Playworks, originally the Goodman Children's Theatre, was already giving performances for young people in 1925. Museums are constantly creating exciting permanent and temporary kid-oriented exhibits, and the city's performing arts for youngsters are as varied as the award-winning ones for adults.

Chicago is also blessed by Mother Nature. Miles of beaches and parks stretch along Lake Michigan, and the new Millennium Park adds another natural touch to the urban landscape. Increasingly, there is no age limit to enjoy any of these wonders, because more and more places have spaces where even infants find activities to stimulate their developing brains. Open the book to any page and find a helpful description of a kid-friendly attraction, with age ratings to ensure it's right for your family, phone numbers and Web addresses for further information, smart tips to help you make the most of your visit, and family-friendly eats nearby.

GETTING TO KNOW CHICAGO

Locating places to have fun doesn't have to be a chore. You can look in the handy directories in the back of this book to find an attraction that's right for you. The directory called "Something for Everyone" gives attractions by subject matter, while "All Around Town" lets you search by neighborhood. Or just leaf through the 68 listings, and pick a place that interests you. It's not hard to figure out where each is located.

Chicago is divided into a grid. Although the system is not entirely foolproof, ground zero for Chicago addresses is the intersection of State and Madison streets. Each block going north and south, east and west, increases the street numbers by 100. You won't need a compass to navigate, though, since Lake Michigan is always to the east.

Getting where you want to go in the city may be easy, but finding a parking space or reasonably priced parking garage can be a challenge. For information on public transportation, especially for a copy of the well-organized "Bus & Rail Map," contact the Chicago Transit Authority (tel. 312/836-7000, www.transitchicago.com). The map clearly indicates how to get to family-friendly activities using CTA buses, L trains, Metra commuter trains, and PACE suburban buses. Each L train line has a color code. If your children are old enough, have them help you make the travel plans. Strollers are accepted on public transportation but must remain folded. Most L stations do not have elevators, so that means lugging strollers up and down stairs. The CTA offers discounted visitor passes, and mid-June–Labor Day, up to 3 children under 12 ride free on Metra trains with a fare-paying adult. There are also free trolleys to a number of places.

For a sightseeing tour, try an authentic double-decker bus or trolley (tel. 773/648-5000 for both, www.chicagodoubledecker.com and www.chicagotrolley.com), which make stops around the city. For the price of an all-day pass ($20 ages 12 and up, $10 children 3–11), you can get on and off as often as you want.

You can also have fun and learn a lot by venturing out on your own in Chicago's ethnic communities. Stroll along Devon Avenue (between 2200 and 3000 west), a multicultural neighborhood of stores selling saris from India and nesting dolls from Russia, kosher bakeries, and Asian restaurants. Or pass through the ornate gateway at the entrance to Chinatown (Wentworth Ave. and Cermak Rd.) to discover places to shop for Buddhas and paper lanterns and to have a tasty meal while your child learns to use chopsticks.

WAYS TO SAVE MONEY

The prices listed in the book are regular adult, student (with ID), and kids' prices; children under the ages specified are free. It always pays to ask at the ticket booth whether any discounts are offered for a particular status or affiliation (but don't forget to bring your ID), and you can often find coupons in local newspapers.

If you plan to see several major attractions in a short time, you can save 50% with a CityPass (tel. 707/256-0490, www.citypass.net), which covers admission to five museums and the Sears Skydeck over nine days. The Chicago Public Library has a limited number of Check Us Out cards, valid for free family admission to nine museums in two weeks; Art Access cards, good for free family admission to the Museum of Contemporary Art; and Imagination on Loan cards, valid for free admission to the Chicago Children's Museum. These cards are very popular, so you may have to visit the library more than once to get one. In addition, the major museums each have a day of the week when admission is free. And if your family is interested in a particular institution, consider joining. Members generally get discounts, invitations to special events, and newsletters.

WHEN TO EXPLORE CHICAGO

Like all gardens, Chicago changes with the seasons. Though this book describes only permanent activities, many special events are held throughout the year. Printer's Row Book Fair (Dearborn St., between Congress Pkwy. and Polk St., tel. 312/987–9896), late May–early June, has lots of activities and performances for kids. Taste of Chicago (Grant Park, along Columbus Dr. between Jackson and Randolph Sts., tel. 312/744–3315), late June–early July, has kid-friendly, hands-on projects, entertainment, and, of course, food. Ravinia Kids Concerts (Lake Cook and Green Bay Rds., Highland Park, tel. 847/266–5100) presents music and dance programs by well-known performers early June–early September. The 10-day Chicago International Children's Film Festival (Facets Multi-Media, 1517 W. Fullerton Ave., tel. 773/281–9075), which shows animated films, shorts, and features from around the world, takes place in mid-October. The Children's Humanities Festival (tel. 312/661–1028) presents programs at various locations in early November. The lighting of Chicago's Christmas tree (Daley Center Plaza, Washington St. between Dearborn and Clark Sts.) and the Christmas parade (State St.) are held on Thanksgiving weekend (tel. 312/744–33150). For information on other events, contact the Mayor's Office of Special Events (tel. 312/744–3315) or the Visitor Information Centers (Chicago Cultural Center, 78 E. Washington St., tel. 800/487–2446; Historic Water Tower, 806 N. Michigan Ave., tel. 800/487–2448).

And when you're deciding when to go, remember that the hours listed in this book are an attraction's basic hours, not necessarily those applicable on holidays. Some sights are closed when schools are closed, but others add extra hours on those days. It's always best to check.

FOLLOW THE YELLOW BRICK ROAD

Chicago has another claim to fame. It's where L. Frank Baum wrote *The Wonderful Wizard of Oz*. As a tribute to the beloved book, a larger-than-life statue of the Tin Man stands in Oz Park (2021 N. Burling St.). So tap your heels together, and flip the pages of this book to follow the Tin Man as he tumbles from one end of Chicago to the other. Together, you can get blown away finding lots of wonderful ways to have fun in the Windy City. And if you look carefully while you're turning the pages, you'll see that the Tin Man, just like the city, has a big heart.

When you're safely back home after your adventures, we'd love to hear from you. What did you and your children think about the places we recommend? Have you found other places we should include? Send us your ideas via e-mail (c/o editors@fodors.com, specifying *Around Chicago with Kids* on the subject line) or snail mail (c/o Around Chicago with Kids, Fodor's Travel Publications, 280 Park Avenue, New York, NY 10017). In the meantime, get ready, get set, and go have a great time seeing Chicago with your kids!

—Nancy Maes

ADLER PLANETARIUM AND ASTRONOMY MUSEUM

68

Change in the universe is slow, but change in the way we view it and understand it doesn't have to be. This six-decades-old planetarium has kept up with the times, offering stargazers both low-tech and high-tech means of exploring the heavens.

Start in the History of Astronomy Galleries to see items used over the centuries to explore the universe. Kids interested in astronomy the way it used to be can step into the restored Atwood Sphere. Predating the 1930 planetarium, the big steel sphere was once part of the Chicago Academy of Sciences. Small holes allow light in, simulating Chicago's night sky in 1913, complete with the movements of planets. If your children want a splendid view of Chicago and its sky today, check out the semicircular, glass-enclosed addition, which overlooks Lake Michigan; a ground-level telescope yields a close-up look at celestial objects. The Gateway to the Universe will transport them in a different way. Here they can take a space walk, discovering the roles of light, gravity, motion, and energy.

HEY, KIDS! Do you know what "spaghettifying" means? No, it's not some horrifying pasta experiment. It's a phenomenon that happens near a black hole. To get a feel for it, head to the wall of mirrors in the Sky Pavilion. The reflection of your body will look long and skinny, like a strand of spaghetti. That's what you would really look like if you got too close to the gravity of a black hole. We *don't* recommend trying the real thing!

At other exhibits children put on 3-D glasses and experience the Milky Way as though they were there (which, of course, they are) and step into a solar observatory. For the latest news about the universe, they go to visualization stations for live hookups with NASA experts or perhaps with an orbiting space station visible on a large, saucer-shape screen. Sophisticated sky shows are in store in the Zeiss Sky Theater, here since the planetarium opened. But the museum's pièce de résistance is the domed StarRider Theater, the first of its kind. Using the same technology used to train pilots and astronauts in flight simulators, it enables kids, and adults, to imagine themselves as colonists on Mars. First, audience members make decisions, such as where to set up a colony and what kind of shelter to build. Next, would-be colonists recline in their chairs and "depart" on a thrilling customized adventure, watching as 60 3-D images a second are projected onto the ceiling.

And when all the wizardry is over, you can just gaze at the night sky in silence.

EATS FOR KIDS

An expanse of windows overlooks Lake Michigan and the sky above at **Galileo's,** the planetarium's restaurant. It serves reasonably priced pizzas, pastas, and salads with an upscale touch and, for fussy eaters, hot dogs and peanut butter sandwiches.

KEEP IN MIND Very young children may be more frightened than enthralled by the sky shows, and StarRider, in particular, may be overwhelming. If you decide to take youngsters to see one of the shows, describe the experience to them beforehand and be ready for some hand-holding.

AMERICAN GIRL PLACE

Mirroring the expansion of the country it chronicles, the American Girls enterprise has expanded by leaps and bounds. This three-level store, the first of its kind, is a destination for any girl who loves the American Girls, and many a young lady dresses up and brings her doll along to share the experience.

At the heart of American Girls is an immensely popular series of books about seven girls (Felicity, Josefina, Kirsten, Addy, Samantha, Kit, and Molly) living in different places and eras of American history, from Colonial Williamsburg to World War II. While revealing nitty-gritty details about growing up during that time, the stories go beyond simple history lessons, enabling young readers to discover similarities between their own lives and the lives of these strong-willed, compassionate girls.

Out of these books, a merchandising empire has grown. Each character comes as a much-coveted doll with her own wardrobe and accoutrements, which are displayed in a glass

EATS FOR KIDS Overlooking the historic Water Tower, the fancy second-floor **Cafe** serves food inspired by the books. Nibble on Kit's heart-shape cheese sandwiches or Josefina's corn muffins. Lunch and tea are $16 each, and dinner is $18 (reservations required). Also see Hancock Observatory.

HEY, KIDS! Children long ago didn't have very many material possessions of their own. Not only did most girls have only one outfit for their doll, but they had only one doll. The American Girls themselves derived pleasure from simple games and activities. See if you can follow their example and limit the number of American Girl products that you "must have." Remember that Felicity loved just going to her father's store; she didn't have to buy stuff.

case. Plenty of other items can be seen (and purchased) here, too. Girls can join the American Girls Club, acquire wardrobes that match their AG dolls, or thumb through books for and about today's girls.

American Girl Place is more than just an elegant store, however. It's also a place to learn about America's history. For example, dioramas for each doll are complete down to the smallest objects, such as Kit's old-fashioned typewriter in her attic bedroom. A cozy 150-seat theater presents a musical revue for children 7 and up (reservations required), featuring young girls in the roles of the seven brave characters. (After a highly successful first review, a new one, called *Circle of Friends,* opened at the end of 2001; others will follow, but the inspiration will remain the same.) Their stories should help to remind your children that the American Girls are not just about buying as much as you can, but also about the importance of believing in your strengths and following your heart.

KEEP IN MIND The pressure will be on to spend a lot of money here. Discuss spending limits with your kids before you make the trip, not after they've seen all the wonderful merchandise. Or encourage them to bring their own money. You might even want to discuss how much a dollar would have bought in the days of their favorite American Girls and then let them see how far a dollar will go at today's American Girl Place.

Art might never intimidate your children again after they visit the Art Institute, a pioneer in children's art programs.

Start at the Kraft Education Center, where the exhibit Telling Images: Stories in Art displays six works from different cultures and periods, as well as hands-on activities that help kids understand them. (The exhibit was designed by architect Stanley Tigerman, with input from some playful and inventive youngsters.) For example, kids can look at a montage by Martina Lopez, who used a computer to superimpose old family photographs on a mural landscape, and then have fun placing magnetized photographs on another landscape. They can push a button to hear about a 16th-century Indian Vishnu statue; try a computer game about people in the painting *Train Station,* which illustrates the South's segregation laws; or play with puppets depicting characters in the painting *St. George Killing the Dragon*. In fall 2002 the exhibit will be replaced by Looking to See, which will again combine plenty of hands-on, kid-friendly activities alongside works depicting people, everyday objects, and spiritual life.

EATS FOR KIDS The museum's **Court Cafeteria** has pizzas, hot dogs, and macaroni. The children's menu at **Bennigan's** (150 S. Michigan Ave., tel. 312/427–0577) includes a choice of chicken fingers, a hot dog, macaroni and cheese, or a cheeseburger, all served with fries. **Cosí** (116 S. Michigan Ave., tel. 312/263–6595) serves gourmet sandwiches, thin-crust pizzas, and all the ingredients to make your own s'mores over a small flame brought to the table.

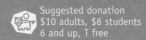

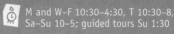
Also in the Kraft Education Center, free weekend artist demonstrations might teach about printmaking, drawing from a model, or other techniques. At drop-in workshops, kids might create a collage, a decorated paper plate, or other project inspired by artworks here. The center also offers storytelling, puppet shows, and dance programs, and has a cozy reading room. Changing exhibits of original children's-book illustrations, from fairy-tale paintings to cartoonlike drawings, show how pictures tell stories.

To best view the "adult" galleries, take a guided or self-guided tour, the latter thanks to free, lively guidebooks. The most popular one, called "On Guard!," covers the Art of Arms and Armor collection. Brochures reveal interesting facts and ask children questions about artworks. The Ancient Art gallery also appeals to kids, who can use a computerized multimedia guide called "Cleopatra." The Thorne Rooms' miniature interiors show where everyone from kings to early Americans lived.

HEY, KIDS! The more than 700 colorful glass paperweights here are pretty amazing, but even more amazing is that they belonged to one person, who donated them to the museum. How do they compare with your collections? If you had that many beautiful objects, would you let everyone see them?

KEEP IN MIND If you and your family want to explore the museum a little bit more, buy a copy of the lively book *Behind the Lions: A Family Guide to the Art Institute of Chicago*, available at the museum store. (The title refers to the two lion sculptures at the entrance to the museum.) The book discusses approximately 60 artworks, includes color photographs, and contains instructions for art projects that children can make with simple items found around the house.

BRONZEVILLE CHILDREN'S MUSEUM

During the 1920s, the Bronzeville neighborhood, on Chicago's South Side between 31st and 39th streets and State Street and King Drive, was like a city within the city. Black culture, commerce, churches, and politics flourished. So it's not surprising that Peggy Montes chose the name Bronzeville for the children's black-history museum she founded in 1998. Though it currently occupies a modest space on a suburban shopping mall's lower level, she has big plans to one day relocate it to Bronzeville, which is being revitalized. Space is limited, but the ideas of Montes, a former teacher, are not.

The museum mounts one exhibit at a time, changing about every four months, but each one is chock-full of things to do. Young visitors here can take a guided tour to discover the important contributions of varied African-Americans through equally varied and engaging activities: make-believe play, computer games, videos and films, hands-on crafts, and a song written especially for the occasion.

EATS FOR KIDS The Evergreen Plaza shopping mall has a **food court** (tel. 773/445–8900) with an abundance of choices. You can opt for McDonald's, steaks, pizzas, Asian and Greek dishes, ice cream, and other snacks and sweets.

KEEP IN MIND Learning about the history of black Americans doesn't have to stop after a visit to the museum. Use this as an opportunity to discuss issues of race with your children, as appropriate to their age. With younger kids, get library books about African-Americans past and present who should be better known. With older children, be prepared to discuss weightier topics, such as shameful events in our country's history or the fact that so many textbooks over the years have failed to mention many accomplished African-Americans.

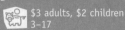
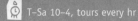

For example, during the exhibit The Underground Railroad: Blacks and Whites Together, children could try on shackles; learn "Follow the Drinking Gourd," a spiritual that helped guide runaway slaves; and put together a puzzle of Harriet Tubman—all while learning about the Underground Railroad. In How Blacks Built the West, the history lesson may have changed, but the fun didn't. Young visitors could dress as cowboys and cowgirls, spin a lasso, shop at a western-style store, and watch a short film about amazing black rodeo cowboys. For an exhibit about the botanist, agricultural chemist, and peanut expert George Washington Carver, kids could see a diorama of a peanut growing underground, listen to a talking peanut, pretend to conduct experiments, and take home a recipe for peanut butter. In yet another exhibit, called African Americans in Aviation: Up and Away, kids could play a flight-simulation game, make their own paper-and-Popsicle-stick plane, and learn about two African-American pilots who had to go to France to learn to fly. No matter what your children's skin color, they can learn about people and exploits that deserve recognition while also having a great time.

HEY, KIDS! How many famous black Americans you can name? Make a list, and ask your parents to add the ones that they know. Then, to see how much you learn at this children's museum, make another list after your visit. Bet you'll be surprised at how much more you know!

BROOKFIELD ZOO

Your family can have an almost "you are there" experience at this 216-acre zoo, where animals live in naturalistic settings. And "there" could be anywhere on the planet.

Tropic World transports you to a rain forest, where some trees are 50 feet tall and regular thunderstorms drop rain on creatures from South America, Asia, and Africa. (Don't worry: you won't get wet on the walkways overlooking them.) Take a make-believe safari through Habitat Africa to discover how the Ituri people, animals, and plants share a West African forest. Or walk through a swamp with a squishy-feeling walkway to see salamanders, screech owls, and other animals of the Illinois wetlands. (Don't worry here, either; you don't need mud boots.) Journey to the west coast of South America at the Living Coast: A World of Surprising Connections, and learn about moon jellies, small sharks, and sea turtles. The recorded sounds of gurgling water and of whales and other creatures as well as beams of shifting light make you feel like you're underwater. The Fragile Kingdom takes you to Africa and Asia, home to Siberian tigers, snow leopards, jaguars, and lions. At the Baboon Island

EATS FOR KIDS The zoo has lots of concessions and restaurants: the **Eco-Café** (organic snacks), **Cafe Olé** (Mexican), **Safari Stop Restaurant** (burgers, hot dogs, pizzas, and chicken sandwiches), **Backyard Barbecue, La Gran Cocina** (South American specialties, plus a salad bar, stir-fries, and pizzas), **Bocaditos** (also South American), **Tonga Hut** (fried chicken, subs), **Tropic World Refreshments, Nyani Lodge,** and the **Bear Gardens Café.** Most eateries have AniMeals—with a hot dog or hamburger, fruit, and a gift.

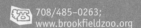

1st Ave. and 31st St., Brookfield

$7 ages 12 and up, $3.50 children 3–11; Oct–Mar T and Th free; some attractions extra

Memorial Day–Labor Day, daily 9:30–6; early Sept–late May, daily 10–5

708/485-0263; www.brookfieldzoo.org

All ages

display, your children can learn about the research that's going on and even help to gather some. Along the ¼-mile Salt Creek Wilderness trail, which circles a 4-acre lake, you'll see swans and other waterfowl, turtles, frogs, and raccoons. At the lake's north end is the Dragonfly Marsh, and the popular Seven Seas Panorama presents a dolphin show daily.

At the Hamill Family Zoo, kids can dress up as animals or play zookeeper, veterinarian, or gardener. Babies dig in dirt, snuggle in a padded bird's nest, or touch tiny insects, learning that even small creatures are important. The Rhythm & Roots Festival, comprising music, dance, storytelling, and craft activities from cultures associated with animal exhibits, usually runs Friday–Sunday in summer. The zoo also holds a Teddy Bear Picnic in August, Boo at the Zoo! for Halloween, and Holiday Magic late November–December. Whew!

HEY, KIDS! Play the Quest to Save the Earth game. Labels along a path explain how to play. Choose between environmentally friendly and unfriendly actions. If you choose correctly, you advance. At the end a huge brown globe turns green if you touch it and pledge to support conservation.

KEEP IN MIND There are more than 2,600 animals at the zoo, ranging from aardvarks (like Arthur on the popular PBS show) to zebras. It's hard to see them all, especially if your child is prone to tired feet or you are prone to tired arms. Get a map when you arrive and decide with your family what everyone wants to see the most. If you just don't want to do all that walking, invest in tickets for the Motor Safari.

BUCCANEER PIRATE
ADVENTURE CRUISES

Young would-be pirates don pirate hats and come aboard the *Buccaneer*, a 150-passenger cruise ship resembling a pirate vessel. The boat owes its convincing pirate feel to a Jolly Roger flying overhead, a blue and black exterior, mermaid figurehead on her bow, and trompe l'oeil gun ports and cannons painted along her sides. Some of the interior has a weathered look.

The crew is a motley group dressed in bandannas, striped T-shirts, ragged shirts, and sashes—but no eye patches, since they have to see what they're doing. The captain's clothes are more elegant, including a white shirt with ruffles and a fitted jacket. While there may be a saber or two and a little pirate talk at boarding time, all that gets put aside when it's time to operate the ship.

The vessel sails along the Chicago River to Lake Michigan, while children gaze at Chicago's skyline, perhaps dreaming of all the loot that could be plundered there. Or

HEY, KIDS!
Pirates used the picture of the skull and crossbones to signal a death threat to their enemies. Today the symbol is sometimes used on warning labels for poisons to signal basically the same thing—that consuming it would be life threatening.

KEEP IN MIND Explain to kids the rules of safe behavior on boats before boarding, since pirates have enough dangers to contend with. Running is not permitted, because the decks may be slippery, and there's absolutely no standing on the seats or climbing on the handrails, as no one is supposed to be walking any planks here. Children should listen carefully to the captain when he points out where the life jackets can be found in case of an emergency.

 Wagner Charter Cruise Co. Dock, south side of Chicago River, east of Columbus Dr. bridge

 $12

  May–Sept., Sa 10:30

1–13

630/653–8690;
www.wagnercharter.com

they might be too busy watching a pirate magician perform tricks and make balloon sculptures like swords, which could come in handy if the enemy appears. Kids don't have to wield a sword to come home with booty, however, because they each get a skull and crossbones–decorated bag filled with treasure: a pirate hat, eye patch, and gold doubloons with chocolate inside. Since piracy can make you thirsty, budding buccaneers get a soft drink without having to fight for it.

When the weather is nice, the sides of the ship are open during the 1½-hour cruise, but a transparent protective curtain can be closed when the elements dictate, so it's not too much of an adventure. As the *Buccaneer* returns to shore, young pirates receive diplomas certifying that they have completed and survived the excursion and that they have performed all their duties. Signing the certificate and swearing to live by the pirate's code gives them the right to call themselves scoundrels.

EATS FOR KIDS The kids' food at **Houlihan's** (111 E. Wacker Dr., tel. 312/616–3663) includes hot dogs and grilled-cheese sandwiches served with french fries as well as pizzas. The **Corner Bakery** (360 N. Michigan Ave., tel. 312/236–2400) serves sandwiches with lots of fresh ingredients on a variety of specialty breads (buy a loaf to take home), pizzas, and yummy brownies. The **Shops at North Bridge food court** (520 N. Michigan Ave., tel. 312/327–2300), on the fourth floor, offers a world tour of Italian, Mexican, and Asian food and good old American hot dogs.

CALDWELL WOODS

Native American trails once crossed this area, but in 1829 Billy Caldwell, chief of the Ottawa, Chippewa, and Potowatomi nations, helped negotiate a treaty between the Native Americans and the U.S. government. The tribes agreed to leave the region and move on to lands west of the Mississippi. To thank him for his efforts, the U.S. government granted Caldwell the land that now bears his name and belongs to the Cook County Forest Preserve. Caldwell Woods provides recreation in all seasons. Paths for walking in the woods and along the North Branch of the Chicago River lure families on pleasant spring and fall days. The diverse landscape includes patches of prairie with grasses 6 feet tall, wetlands, and savanna where wildflowers and grasses grow in between scattered trees. There is even room for picnic tables.

In summer, the Whealan Aquatic Center offers something for everyone. Serious swimmers find lanes for doing laps. Girls (and boys) who just want to have fun enjoy a long slide

KEEP IN MIND Since the aquatic center is free, on nice summer days the pool has been known to reach its maximum capacity, after which no one else is allowed to enter. The best way to avoid crowds *and* disappointment is to come early.

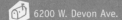

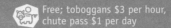
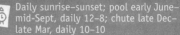

that zigs and zags and then zigzags again before plunging into the water. Youngsters frolic in a play area that looks like a house on stilts with water gushing over it and out of spouts around it. Wee ones like a pool that's just their size, with a mini slide and small sprays of water shooting into the air. An area filled with sand is nearby. And for those who want to relax, there's a grassy area for sunbathing.

Come winter, your children may want to rent a toboggan or bring their own to use on slides constructed from snow and ice. Or they might want to bring a sled or other slippery object to slide down the hills. There's also an outdoor ice-skating rink. It's a far cry from the forest preserve the Native Americans left behind.

EATS FOR KIDS

The pool has a **concession stand** with tables shaded by umbrellas. Another option is **Superdawg Drive-In** (6363 N. Milwaukee Ave., tel. 773/763–0660), which is known not only for hot dogs but also for its giant statues of hot dogs dressed as humans standing on the roof.

HEY, KIDS! You'll have a happier, and maybe even a healthier, time if you follow the safety and courtesy rules at the facilities here. Remember that no running is allowed at the pool and that you have to stand in line and wait your turn at all slides—both at the pool in summer and at the toboggan chute in winter.

CHICAGO BOTANIC GARDEN

These gardens may be "formal," but children don't mind; for them, a visit here is informal and fun. They can discover countless plants—including 5,000 roses—throughout the growing season. Just call or stop at the Gateway Center to find out what's blooming, and pick up a chart of the best viewing times for each area.

The Fruit and Vegetable Garden is an eye-opener for children who think produce grows in plastic at the supermarket, while a beehive shows honey making and pollinating in action. Water-loving kids can walk to the top of the Waterfall Garden and watch water cascade down the hillside or get wet themselves under the Circle Garden fountain's 8-foot-tall arches. In the Children's Garden, kids can cross a bridge over a pond where dwarf cattails grow, lose their way in an evergreen maze, meander through a willow tunnel, and call a sunflower house home.

Although outdoor exhibits, such as one with big bugs made of natural materials, spring up in warm weather, the garden is also worth visiting in winter, when greenhouses,

KEEP IN MIND For a manageable visit to this 385-acre garden, get a map from the information desk and pick the gardens your family most wants to see. Alternatively, take a tram tour, which lets kids cover more ground without getting tired—and probably spot more ducks and geese, too.

HEY, KIDS! Cross the bridge that zigzags across the Japanese Garden, making sure to pay attention to where you're going. (The cement bridge has no railings, and walking straight will land you in the water.) According to the Japanese, traversing this kind of bridge is a good way to lose any evil spirits who may be following you because they can only walk in straight lines. It doesn't work on parents, though.

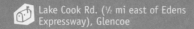

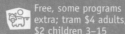

filled with plants from habitats ranging from rain forest to desert, are always warm. Your kids can look for a Venus's-flytrap, which catches insects and makes a meal of them, and all sorts of animal-shape topiaries, including a donkey, an orangutan, a toucan in a tree, and a towering dinosaur. Another greenhouse has food trees, such as banana and coffee plants. On a touch table, children can feel the soft and furry leaves of the panda bear plant and the smooth ones of the aloe vera. The Japanese Garden has pruned trees and stone lanterns shaped to catch the snow.

Other reasons to visit the botanical garden bloom only on selected days. Kids may listen to stories about creatures that fly at night and then take a walk in the woods to see them, or they may learn about roots you can eat and then record their own roots by making a family tree. Day camps, a kids' gardening club, family garden picnics, sleep-overs, Teddy Bear Teas, and the winter holidays' Celebrations festival dot a calendar that's always growing something fun.

EATS FOR KIDS The **Food for Thought Cafe** (Gateway Center, tel. 847/835–3040) offers soups, gourmet salads, and sandwiches, but never fear: Choices for children are available, too. The café is open year-round, but in summer, you can sit on a pleasant patio overlooking water. There are more outdoor tables adjacent to the Rose Garden, where you can buy sandwiches and drinks, and in other garden areas for picnickers.

CHICAGO CHILDREN'S MUSEUM

Hip, hip hooray! This is one of Chicago's best places to play. Three floors of hands-on exhibits turn doing into believing and teach kids about the world, themselves, and others. To plan your day, get a "Guest Guide" at the admissions desk. Your first stop, however, will be obvious. Just inside waits a three-story schooner similar to ones that once sailed Lake Michigan. Children love to climb the rope ladder to the deck, carefully pick their way across a rope bridge to the gangplank, and slide down to the lower level, where there are fish like those that call the lake home. Adults are welcome aboard, too.

The most awesome exhibits are in the 50-foot towers. In the Inventing Lab, kids use their imagination and knowledge of aerodynamics to make airplanes, send them to the tower's top on a conveyor belt, and launch them to see if they soar or plummet. In the other tower, children don raincoats at the Waterways exhibit, manipulate levers, and send water through brightly colored pipes, over waterwheels, and along streams waiting to be dammed. If everyone joins forces and pumps hard enough, water will shoot 50 feet in the air.

EATS FOR KIDS Navy Pier (*see #21*) has many eateries. Dimly lit, out-of-this-world **McDonald's** (tel. 312/832–1640) has occasional laser-light shows. The **Food Court** offers Chinese, Greek, and Italian fare. In the beautiful six-story, glass-domed **Crystal Gardens,** a tropical spot with burbling fountains, you can eat food you've brought from home or purchased here.

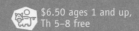
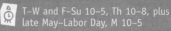
When it's time to engage the mind instead of the muscles, head to Face to Face: Dealing with Prejudice and Discrimination, on the third floor. In Dinosaur Expedition, kids pretend to be paleontologists and dig for dinosaur bones.

Two early childhood exhibits protect little ones from the hubbub. Preschoolers find a city their own size in the third-floor PlayMaze and a piece of the great outdoors in the adjacent Treehouse Trails. Both have enclosed areas filled with toys and other objects that let infants discover the world in their own small ways. Temporary exhibits also include "baby ponds" for little learners.

Creativity is given free reign in the Kraft Artabounds Studio, on the lower level, where drop-in workshops are inspired by museum exhibits, a holiday, or other special event. Temporary exhibits are installed regularly and special activities are added often.

HEY, KIDS! Slide down the xylophone slide, at the entrance to the Inventing Lab, and listen to the music created by your movement. You can look through the transparent slide to see how the xylophone works. The inventor must have quite an imagination, don't you think?

KEEP IN MIND Once you get here, which can be a small adventure in itself (*see* Getting There in Navy Pier), there are enough exhibits and activities to fill up a whole day, but you'll want to pace yourself to avoid over-tired kids. Alternate between active and quiet activities, and take a break for a snack or lunch. If you're lucky, by the end of the day your children will actually be ready to leave the museum and return to reality.

CHICAGO CULTURAL CENTER

When this cultural center was built in 1897, it was called the "People's Palace" because the beautiful block-long building—whose exterior was inspired by Greek and Roman architecture and whose interior was influenced by Italian Renaissance palaces—was funded by the city so that everyone could enjoy the arts free of charge. Many of the spaces on its five floors are worth visiting just to see the splendid ornamentation, including marble, polished brass, stained glass, colored stone, and mother-of-pearl mosaics. Nowadays the center is alive with many styles of music, theater, and dance—all free.

The center puts on children's programs, including workshops and performances, several times a month as well as major festivals four times a year. So you might drop in on a concert of Andean music, a dance program depicting the history and architecture of Chicago, or a cooking class making yummy desserts. During Theater Fever in February, kids can get into the act by learning what it takes to be on stage. They might find out how to prepare for an audition, practice improvisational techniques, create a puppet, or learn how to

EATS FOR KIDS The cultural center has a **Corner Bakery** (tel. 312/201–0805), one in a chain of restaurants found around the city and the suburbs. It serves appetizing sandwiches, some on baguettes; salads; and desserts, including fudge brownies and raspberry bars.

HEY, KIDS! Ask for a free copy of "A Young Person's Guide to the Cultural Center," which has lots of interesting information about the center and games to play, too. With guide in hand, look for the beautiful stained-glass domed ceiling of Preston Bradley Hall and the ceiling in the Grand Army of the Republic Rotunda, encrusted with interesting designs. The booklet challenges you to find designs, precious materials, and quotations in the interior ornamentation and to discover architectural elements.

 78 E. Washington St.

 Free

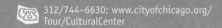 312/744-6630; www.cityofchicago.org/
Tour/CulturalCenter

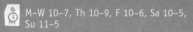 M–W 10–7, Th 10–9, F 10–6, Sa 10–5,
Su 11–5

 All ages

release their inner fool. Activities in the spring are often inspired by a city-wide event, such as a free puppet workshop given in conjunction with Puppetropolis. Hallowed Halls, held in October, might feature activities inspired by *The Wizard of Oz,* such as making flying monkey kites. For one winter holiday program, an actress playing Queen Elizabeth arrived in a horse-drawn carriage, and the ensuing celebration featured a jousting match. A royal time was had by all.

Since adult programs are offered daily, this is also a good place for kids to get a free sample of culture. Noon concerts featuring classical, jazz, folk, and pop are given almost daily, and other regular programs spotlight the cultures of Chicago's sister cities. There is seldom a dull moment at the cultural center, which also houses the Museum of Broadcast Communications (*see* #25). Your children can become familiar with many performing arts genres and with the artists themselves—and, in the process, may discover their own creative abilities.

KEEP IN MIND The cultural center hosts not only performing arts programs but also the visual arts: about a half-dozen temporary exhibits at a time. The artworks generally represent painting, photography, or sculpture but have also included assemblages of objects such as books, razor blades, and shoes; quilt art that included painted images and handwritten texts; and carved wooden animals by a Japanese folk artist. So while you're here, take a walk around to see what catches your and your children's interest.

CHICAGO HISTORICAL SOCIETY

Founded in 1856, the society is the city's oldest cultural institution, though its museum opened later. (It moved to this brick Georgian building in 1932.) But despite its serious-sounding pedigree, it has plenty to interest children. Costumed characters representing well-known historical figures give 20-minute performances in galleries; temporary exhibits feature hands-on activities; special programs take place year-round; and even permanent exhibits, especially on the first floor, are child friendly. In fact, the Hands-On History Gallery was created for kids.

Here youngsters can pretend to be part of the city's past. They can play with paraphernalia fur traders once used and feel different animal pelts. If their legs are long enough, they can climb onto an old-fashioned high-wheeler bicycle. They can try on shirt collars and cuffs or button shoes using a buttonhook. In a corner exhibit about old-fashioned radio programs, they can create sound effects with simple items, such as coconut shells for the clip-clop of horses' hooves and a sheet of metal that, when rattled, resembles a storm.

EATS FOR KIDS The museum restaurant, called **Big Shoulders** (tel. 312/587–7766) after poet Carl Sandburg's description of Chicago as the "City of the Big Shoulders," is a two-story glassed-in space with an outdoor patio. Its menu for little ones includes grilled-cheese sandwiches on millet bread served with roasted potatoes; peanut butter and jelly sandwiches, also on millet bread, with fresh fruit; hamburgers; and pasta.

 Clark St. and North Ave.

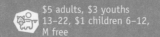 $5 adults, $3 youths 13–22, $1 children 6–12, M free

 M–Sa 9:30–4:30, Su 12–5; Hands-On History M–F 10–2, Sa 11–4:30, Su 12–4:30

 312/642–4600; www.chicagohistory.org

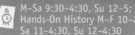 4 and up

The Illinois Pioneer Life Galleries, also on the first floor, present life circa 1818–1850. There are places for spinning and weaving, candle making, blacksmithing, and printing, and people wearing pioneer clothes demonstrate crafts on weekends. Your children can look at old-fashioned instruments and guess what a niddy noddy and a sausage gun were used for. (They measure yarn and shoot meat into sausage casing, respectively.)

In the Chicago History Galleries children can peer into dioramas depicting city history. A film on the Great Chicago Fire of 1871 shows how the city was destroyed and rebuilt. (No one blames Mrs. O'Leary's cow anymore.) Your kids can climb into the cab of the *Pioneer,* a real locomotive from the mid-1800s, and learn how the engineer stopped the train (by putting it in reverse, since it didn't have brakes). And then they'll go full steam ahead again, learning about Chicago's past by reliving it themselves.

HEY, KIDS! Check out the objects that decorate the walls of the museum's lobby. See if you can find a toy truck and sand loader, some juggling equipment, and bottles of Hires Root Beer and the fruit drink Tango-La, both popular beverages in the Chicago of the 1930s.

KEEP IN MIND The film of the Great Chicago Fire is very impressive, but it might be too frightening for some children. Naturally, the subject matter is disturbing, underscored by a soundtrack that includes the crackling of flames and the shouts of people. Children 6 and up can perhaps handle it, but parents should decide if it's appropriate for a particular child.

CHICAGO MERCANTILE EXCHANGE

Neither your child nor you needs to know what sorghum futures are to make a trip to the fourth-floor visitor center here worthwhile. From it, you can see fast and furious trading on the Chicago Mercantile Exchange, which looks like what happens in a preschool class when the teacher leaves the room. Traders wearing brightly colored jackets stand in pits, where they shout, make faces, and wave their arms frenetically. They are all busy trying to buy or sell agricultural products—maybe live cattle, boneless beef, hog bellies, or even dried cocoons—that will be delivered in the future. Luckily, interactive computer screens help you make sense of the apparent nonsense, explaining what's happening using animated characters, photographs of people working on the exchange, and a sense of humor.

The screaming and yelling you hear is called the "open outcry." It's a kind of auction in which one person calls out prices and others shout back that they want to buy. No wonder everyone looks so stressed. Since it's hard to be heard above the crowd, traders use a

KEEP IN MIND If your child enjoys the mercantile exchange, head up to the eighth floor to see more frantic behavior at the International Monetary Market, where foreign currency is traded. The visitor center here is open Monday–Friday 7:15–2.

EATS FOR KIDS On the exchange's first floor, the **Wall Street Deli** (tel. 312/993–3500) has soups, sandwiches, and salads. Choices in the Presidential Towers (555 W. Madison St.) include **Cafe Italia** and **La Marguerita** (tel. 312/902–4600 for both), Italian and Mexican, respectively; **McDonald's** (tel. 312/902–2600); and **My Thai** (tel. 312/669–1999). **Dylan's** (118 Clinton St., tel. 312/876–2008) has American fare. In nice weather, follow the traders outside, and get the specialty of the trucks—perhaps jerk chicken, pizza, pasta, sandwiches, or burritos.

kind of sign language, too. The computer program will help you decipher these hand gestures—which ones mean buy and sell and which ones tell how much to buy and for what price. Kids can even play a game to see if they've learned them correctly. The people in the pit better have, because that's not the place to make mistakes.

Fashion-conscious teens can discover the key to the wardrobe code: Members of the exchange wear red jackets, whereas the people who report the price and quantity of a trade wear blue. Phone clerks, who use hand signals and written notes to communicate between traders and people on the phones, wear gold coats. The clerks wearing green coats with black badges help resolve discrepancies between buyers and sellers. Once your children have soaked up all this background information, have them look back down on the floor. They may find they understand the method to the traders' seeming madness after all.

HEY, KIDS! Children always want to know if the traders are rich. The answer is that it's hard to generalize about traders. Some are rich and some aren't. Some had other professions and needed a change of pace. Some are 25 years old; some are 75. The one thing they seem to have in common is that they wouldn't be happy sitting still—and quiet—in an office. Can you picture yourself as a trader?

CHICAGO MUSIC MART AT DEPAUL CENTER

For almost 75 years, several blocks along South Wabash Avenue were known as "music row" because so many music manufacturers and shops were here, drawing customers from all over the United States. In the 1960s, competition from suburban shopping malls put many businesses out of business. Then in 1993, a renovated historic landmark christened the Chicago Music Mart opened, and the concept of a one-stop place for musicians to shop and meet was reborn.

The mart has an atrium, mahogany storefronts, terrazzo flooring with inlaid marble accents, Prairie-style stenciling, and music for the ears. Any child who is a musician, wants to be a musician, wants to know about musicians, or just likes to listen to music will find the Music Mart a perfect place to explore. It's filled with all sorts of music-related stores, including ones carrying stringed instruments, percussion instruments, or pianos; a shop that focuses on ways to make music electronically; and CD and tape stores galore. And kids are always welcome to try the instruments.

EATS FOR KIDS There are several restaurants in the Music Mart. Thai food is the specialty at **My Thai** (tel. 312/986–0999), where kids might like *satay* (meat grilled on a stick), egg rolls, chicken with rice, or noodles. **Sbarro** (tel. 312/663–1070), part of a chain, offers about a half-dozen kinds of pizza. The menu at the **Wall Street Deli** (tel. 312/913–0870) includes club, tuna, roast beef, and ham sandwiches; wraps, including a vegetable version; and one food that almost any kid will eat: potato chips.

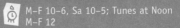

Children can also hear what music sounds like when you're willing to practice a lot. A program called Tunes at Noon presents free concerts, usually held on a stage indoors, where there is seating. During the summer months, weather permitting, they move outdoors, and people sit in seats around the garden or stand. Concerts range from ones by high school and elementary school bands and choral groups to those featuring instrumental music from the Andes, jazz, blues, rock and roll, Latin, big band, and classical—even dance performances. Each day is different. Though there are no concerts on Saturday, it's usually possible to hear the Classical Symphony Orchestra and the Protégé Philharmonic, which are housed in the mart, rehearsing on stage 9–12:30 and 2–5. If your children weren't musicians before coming to the mart, it might inspire them to take up instruments or at least understand music better.

HEY, KIDS! There are many ways to make music, and you can sample a lot of them by visiting stores and trying instruments. If you do decide to take up an instrument, remember that practice makes perfect.

KEEP IN MIND After listening to others and experimenting themselves, children are often inspired to start playing, and many stores here do more than sell instruments, adding rentals and lessons to their repertoire. Tiny fingers can tickle the synthetic ivories at American Music World (tel. 312/786-9600), offering acoustic and digital pianos, organs, and less-expensive keyboards. The Chicago Band & Orchestra Co. (tel. 312/341-0102) carries stringed and wind instruments in children's sizes, with three-month rentals running from $58 to $99. If your kids' commitment isn't strong, opt for the $3 wooden egg shaker.

CHICAGO PLAYWORKS

Playworks—whose full name is actually Chicago Playworks for Families and Young Audiences—has many reasons to be proud. Founded in 1925 as the Goodman Children's Theatre, which later became part of DePaul University, it's Chicago's longest continuously running children's theater as well as one of the first important children's theaters in the United States. Throughout the years it has garnered much praise and many awards for excellence, and current productions, directed by professionals but performed by the remarkably talented students in DePaul's Theatre School, continue to be outstanding. Plays range from traditional fairy tales to "today plays," which deal with contemporary social issues.

The theme one year was "A Season of American Journeys: Dreams Denied and Delayed, Lost and Found." The schedule included one play about two young slaves who travel the Underground Railroad to freedom, and another about children who worked 14-hour days in turn-of-the-20th-century Philadelphia textile mills and about Mother Jones, who led them on a protest march to champion their rights.

HEY, KIDS!

After some performances, you can join in an ice-cream social with cast members. This is a great opportunity to enjoy a yummy treat while talking with actors about the play. Ask a parent to find out the details by calling the theater.

EATS FOR KIDS
Artists Cafe (412 S. Michigan Ave., tel. 312/939–7855) serves simple favorites and has outdoor seating. **Standing Room Only Chicago** (610 S. Dearborn St., tel. 312/360–1776) has burgers alongside healthier choices. Eat outside or in, where sports memorabilia includes 15 feet of wall from the old Chicago Stadium. **Edwardo's** (521 S. Dearborn St., tel. 312/939–3366) is part of a chain known for stuffed and deep-dish pizzas. See the Rosenbaum ARTiFACT Center for more ideas.

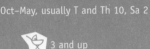
You can expect the costumes and stage design to be as elaborate and inventive as the plays themselves. For example, a recent production of *Jungalbook,* based on Rudyard Kipling's *The Jungle Book,* took place in a contemporary urban setting. The actors who portrayed animal roles wore tattered jeans, baggy pants, and black leather. Some even rode skateboards. Playing out the drama on a super-duper jungle gym, they used fight choreography that would have thrilled any martial arts fan. The result was a very high "cool" quotient that made this story about the importance of defining one's own identity relevant to the lives of kids in the new millennium.

Other Playworks presentations have included *This Is Not a Pipe Dream,* about the childhood of surrealist artist René Magritte, complete with striking visual images that recall his art, and *The Yellow Boat,* about a young boy who developed AIDS from a blood transfusion and found solace in art. The subject may sound morbid, but in fact it was a celebration of the joy of his life. For those not inclined to new dramas, there are also plenty of fairy tales with happy endings.

KEEP IN MIND Not all plays are appropriate for all ages, and you can't always judge what a production will be like by its name. It's best to inquire about the play beforehand so you can decide if it's right for your child. One or two performances of each production are interpreted in American Sign Language.

CHICAGO WHITE SOX

L ittle Leaguers meet the Major League at Comiskey Park, where it's not just the Chicago White Sox and their opponents who play. Kids can play here, too, thanks to several special programs and days offered at the stadium.

Kids who come to any of the team's 81 home games can get in their own practice time at a free area called FUNdamentals, inside Gate 3. It's batter up at the batting cages, where children can try for a home run, or they can practice their fastball at the pitching cages. There's also an area for running bases, so how about pretending to steal a base or slide into home? Instructors are former college coaches and players and even former pro players. Parents are welcome to join in and learn how to teach their kids about batting stances, glove work, and the dynamics of pitching.

Some Sunday games bring even more excitement. Called Willy Wonka Kid's Days, in honor of the boy who got to visit the chocolate factory, they provide an up-close and personal

KEEP IN MIND Balls may be lost for good when they get hit into the crowded stands, but naturally you'll want to make sure your children won't be. Since it's easy to get separated amid the hustle and bustle, you can get your kids ID bracelets that include identification and seat locations. Just stop at one of the Guest Relations booths, behind home plate on the 100, 300, and 500 levels.

treat for only $1. White Sox players are on hand to sign autographs for kids only, and after the game, no matter what the score, kids can circle the bases on the very field where the White Sox play. To top it off, children receive some Willy Wonka candy after their all-American experience. Other promotional days, such as Glove and Bat days, yield the free stuff kids treasure. Kaleidoscope Corners, held on Saturdays and Sundays seven times a summer, let kids play baseball trivia games, color pictures of baseball players, or have their faces painted, perhaps with the White Sox logo. Some Saturday evenings bring a celebration of fireworks set to music, whether the Sox win or lose.

The main event, of course, is the game itself, but even something as simple as singing along to "Take Me Out to the Ballgame," part of the traditional seventh-inning stretch, can make the game memorable and exhilarating. In the end, a baseball game here isn't just sport; it's a social experience.

EATS FOR KIDS
Concession stands serve traditional ballpark food, such as hot dogs, peanuts, and Cracker Jacks as well as chicken fingers and pizza. The **Kids Corner,** on the main concourse, has a children's menu that includes peanut butter and jelly sandwiches as well as a play area.

HEY, KIDS! If you get too hot, don't worry. There's an open-air, outfield shower—just like the one at the old Comiskey Park—which you can stand under with all your clothes on. You can also step into the Rain Room, where a mist fills the air like a rain forest—only not as warm. Located on the center-field concourse, both are open from 1½ hours before game time until the end of the game and are never crowded.

DIVERSEY MINIATURE GOLF

Why choose this course over other Chicago miniature links? Simply put, because it's one of the kindest, gentlest courses around. Many families with young children play here because it's never very crowded and you won't be pressured to play quickly by the golfers behind you, a plus when young children are just getting a grasp of the game. Another plus is the setting: a lovely tree-shaded area of Lincoln Park with a small adjacent play area. It's next to a harbor where boats are docked, and you can see the Chicago skyline in the distance. The course has enough difficult obstacles to keep older children challenged and some simple ones for novices to conquer. Somehow even the littlest players manage to push the ball around a bit and get it into the hole willy-nilly, to the enjoyment of all.

Obstacles aren't big and fancy, but rather small and not too intimidating. Some holes here are pretty straightforward. You might have to hit a ball through a space at the bottom of a barn or lighthouse, around an S-curve, across a bridge, or through tunnels. Other holes

KEEP IN MIND Miniature golf does have rules, so it's best to explain them to all players before you begin. To manage your children's sometimes inevitable frustration, you might want to tailor the rules to suit. Setting a maximum number of strokes can be a blessing or a curse, depending on the child. Younger children might need a little rule-bending to enable them to get the ball in the hole before their next birthday. For older kids, it might be more important to ensure that everyone adheres to the rules, so no one feels cheated. Hopefully, the fun will outweigh any frustration.

141 W. Diversey Pkwy.

312/742-7929

$6 ages 13 and up, $5 children 12 and under

Mar–Oct, daily 6 AM–11 PM; Nov–Feb, daily 7 AM–9 PM; hrs may vary based on weather

2 and up

have animated obstacles, including a windmill and stoplight that both have moving blades to avoid. On one hole, the aim is to get the ball into one of the cars of a turning Ferris wheel, which then whisks the ball around and deposits it on the other side. One of the hardest, however, requires hitting a ball up a ramp and through a small hole leading to a lower level. If the ball doesn't make it into the hole, it just keeps rolling back, so it's easy for scores to rise. But regardless of who gets the lowest score, everybody wins here in an atmosphere that isn't highly competitive.

After the game, winners can celebrate their victory and high scorers can forget their defeat at the adjacent playground. It's filled with swings, ramps, a bridge and tunnel, and a rope net shaped like a spider web ready to tangle the unsuspecting. For another diversion, kids can check out the adults honing their non–miniature golf skills at the double-decker driving range next door.

EATS FOR KIDS
Next to the miniature golf course is a **Subway** (248 W. Diversey Pkwy., tel. 773/281–1212) featuring sandwiches and smoothies. There are outdoor tables in the shade and lots of grassy areas to sit. For nearby restaurant choices, see the Lincoln Park Zoo.

HEY, KIDS! Remember that doing well in miniature golf is a mixture of skill and luck. It's fun to keep score, but don't take the outcome too seriously. Even Tiger Woods loses sometimes. It's being a good sport that always makes you a winner.

DUPAGE CHILDREN'S MUSEUM

Now that this museum is settled into its new location, with double the amount of space, there's twice as much fun to be had. The museum and its hands-on exhibits are divided not by walls—so you can easily keep on eye on your children, wherever they are—but into six themed "neighborhoods." And unlike at some other museums, infants aren't confined to the outskirts. Three Young Explorers areas are next door to areas where older kids can learn firsthand about arts, math, and science.

Some kids gravitate to the Construction House, where they can use saws, hammers, and other real tools on projects—from sawing wood to building a chair for a Beanie Baby. Parents needn't worry about safety. Tools and equipment are scaled to fit small hands, children wear safety goggles, and staff members and volunteers are on hand to help. Tiny tots can become do-it-yourselfers, too, by hammering golf tees into Styrofoam and building with soft blocks.

HEY, KIDS!
Check out the secret tunnel under the WaterFlow table. If you crawl through it, you can pop up inside a clear dome that looks like a giant bubble and be right in the middle of all the splashing—without getting wet.

KEEP IN MIND Children have their own ways of playing at the museum. Some get caught up in one exhibit and want to stay there the whole time, whereas others want to try everything. Even if you are restless or, conversely, engrossed in something, try to follow your child's lead. Ultimately, you'll both probably enjoy the museum more that way. Check out the Parent's Resource Center for more information on raising children.

301 N. Washington St., Naperville

 $5.50 ages 1 and up, special activities free–$1

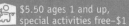 T–W and F–Sa 9–5, Th 9–8, Su 12–5

630/637–8000;
www.dupagechildrensmuseum.org

 3 mths–11 yrs

Older kids can do ExpAIRiments in the Air Works area, where they can wave a special wand to blow a pipe organ and make air socks billow. For a full-body experience they can venture into a wind tunnel. Or they can discover more about Mother Nature at WaterWays; here they can use sandbags to stop the rush of a waterfall and discover what floats and what doesn't. Waterproof aprons are furnished to keep clothes dry. While older children play with shadows and lights in Creativity Connections, infants can enjoy black, white, and red patterns to stimulate their young brains, look at themselves in mirrors, and change the color of a light's filter to see themselves in a whole new perspective.

A variety of special activities inspired by the exhibits are scheduled regularly. Budding artists can make works out of paper, clay, sand, or plastic forks and spoons. Little builders might create a shelter using poles, some string, and a blanket. Family workshops (registration required) include Goopy and Gushy Kidworks, featuring messy art and science projects for a child and an adult partner to share.

EATS FOR KIDS The museum has an **eating area** with vending machines and a microwave, but there are also plenty of child-friendly restaurants, including well-known fast-food joints, nearby. For a change, try pizza at **Lou Malnati's** (131 W. Jefferson St., tel. 630/717–0700), in a former firehouse; pasta at **Noodles and Company** (207 S. Washington St., tel. 630/369–3332); or Chinese food at **Mulan** (200 E. 5th Ave., tel. 630/718–9589).

DUSABLE MUSEUM OF AFRICAN AMERICAN HISTORY

In 1961 Margaret T. Burroughs, cofounder of the National Conference of Negro Artists, started this museum in her home, and in 1973, it moved here, to this former administration building in Washington Park. The museum's exhibits and programs explore the history of black Americans and their African origins and celebrate their culture, past and present.

One such exhibit is the re-created office of Harold Washington, Chicago's first black mayor, who died while in office. Notice the black carved wood stool, like ones given to chieftains in Ghana. (These stools are traditionally blackened when their owner dies.) You can also watch a video that highlights Washington's career.

The permanent collection has more than 10,000 pieces of African-American and African art, displayed on a rotating basis. Ask to see *Freedom Now*, by Robert Ames, in the auditorium. The 8½-foot by 10-foot wood carving depicts aspects of black history from pre-slave-trade Africa to the United States in 1963.

EATS FOR KIDS The museum's location in Washington Park makes it a beautiful place for a picnic. The **CAM Food Court** (5758 S. Maryland St., tel. 773/834–8782), on the second floor of the Center for Advanced Medicine, is open weekdays 7–5. Food stations in the gray and burgundy ultramodern setting offer deli foods, pizzas, wraps, salads, stir-fries, yogurt, and smoothies. There is no problem pleasing kids at **Leona's** (1236 53rd St., tel. 773/363–2600), part of a chain, because pizza's on the menu. For other choices, see the Harold Washington Playlot Park.

 740 E. 56th Pl.

 $3 ages 14 and up, $2 students 14 and up, $1 children 6–13, Su free

M–Sa 10–5, Su 12–5

773/947–0600; www.dusablemuseum.org

Varies by exhibit

In addition, temporary exhibits are regularly displayed, lasting for about six months. Among the exhibits that have really appealed to kids was Black Inventions, which displayed objects invented by African-Americans, including potato chips, the golf tee, the fountain pen, the ironing board, the traffic light, and the Super Soaker water gun.

Finally, there are various programs that children might like: Celebrating the Dream and the King Day Celebration, both in January; the Arts and Crafts Family Festival and the Penny Cinema (1¢), both in July; and, in December, Adorned Trees, featuring trees decorated with objects recalling black people and the places they live; How to Celebrate Kwanza; and Kid's New Year's Eve, for which many boys wear tuxedos and girls wear fancy party dresses. On some Saturdays from April to June, workshops let kids make such items as dolls, banners, and masks. Most programs are free or carry a small charge.

HEY, KIDS! You probably won't need much persuading to go visit the museum's gift shop. But this one is interesting as much for what it is as for what is in it. The indoor store is actually a log cabin similar to one built in the 1770s by fur trader Jean Baptist Point du Sable, a black man credited with being Chicago's first non–Native American resident.

KEEP IN MIND If the museum doesn't engage your kids at first, ask leading questions. Have them compare the images of African-Americans in the art-works here to those they see on TV. Challenge your kids to figure out what various African objects were used for, since most were functional.

ELI'S CHEESECAKE WORLD

Eli's cheesecakes were created as desserts for Eli's The Place for Steak in Chicago, but word spread about how tasty they are. Now they're found all over the country and as far away as Hong Kong and Iceland, giving credence to the name Eli's Cheesecake World. Almost as good as eating Eli's cheesecakes, however, is touring the bakery where they originate.

Except for the white paper cap like those worn by employees—mandatory for everyone who tours the bakery—it's hard to know what to wear. In the baking room the temperature feels tropical. Here you can taste the crust, either chocolate or shortbread, which is cooked before the batter is dropped into the pan. A conveyor belt then moves the cakes through a tunnel-shape oven, and they are put on the bottom of a cooling rack that spirals slowly up two stories. When the cakes reach the top two hours later, they're cool enough to take out of the pan. In the background you'll hear the cling-clang of empty baking pans sliding off a conveyor belt into a container.

KEEP IN MIND The price of cheesecakes in the store at Eli's Cheesecake World is less than what you'll find elsewhere. Ones with slight imperfections are even better bargains, so why not buy two? Your family will no doubt want seconds of these seconds.

HEY, KIDS! To see who else likes Eli's cheesecake, look at the photos on the wall in the café/store. You'll see one of Jay Leno at the bakery, another of Mickey Mouse (a true cheese lover) eating a slice, and the 2,000-pound cheesecake baked for former President Clinton's inauguration in Washington, D.C. Now that would be a little big even for a teenager.

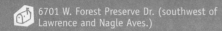

6701 W. Forest Preserve Dr. (southwest of Lawrence and Nagle Aves.)

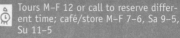

Tours M–F 12 or call to reserve different time; café/store M–F 7–6, Sa 9–5, Su 11–5

773/736–3417; www.elicheesecake.com

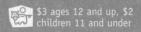

$3 ages 12 and up, $2 children 11 and under

5 and up

From here the cakes are frozen and then frozen some more. Though most of the employees wear white, some are dressed in dark parkas so they can tolerate the freezers. After a brief stint in a cool room, where the cakes are decorated by hand, they return to the freezer before a machine cuts them and puts a piece of paper between each slice, ready for some lucky buyer.

If the tour whets your family's appetite, stop at the café, which carries some 20 cheesecake flavors for sale by the slice—perhaps White Chocolate Raspberry Swirl, Oh My! Mud Pie, Peanut Butter Blast, or Toffee Talk, made with Heath Bar pieces. If you're with a group tour of 20, or if you request it, your child can decorate a slice of plain or chocolate-chip cheesecake, the company's all-time favorite flavors. Except for the noon tour, for which you can walk in, tours should be scheduled two weeks in advance. Special children's activities throughout the year include performances and cooking classes.

EATS FOR KIDS If you're actually hungry after your visit to Eli's Cheesecake World, there is a **McDonald's** (6400 W. Montrose Ave., Harwood Heights, tel. 708/867–1600) nearby. If you don't mind driving a bit, you can go to the **Superdawg Drive-In** (*see* Caldwell Woods) for a slice of Chicago folklore.

EMERALD CITY THEATRE COMPANY

You're definitely not in Kansas anymore at this children's theater company. Its name is indeed a reference to *The Wonderful Wizard of Oz*, written by L. Frank Baum while he was living in Chicago, but it's also a promise of where performances will take young theatergoers. Imaginative productions lead children down the Yellow Brick Road to experience extraordinary adventures and magical moments. Though the company's current home is the modern Apollo Theater—with 400 stadium-style seats and good sight lines—different performance venues have been used over the years. The constant is that anything can happen and usually does.

There are five productions each season, some of which are original works written for the company. One included a new superhero named Captain Virtue, inspired by King Arthur. This good guy sprang from the pages of a contemporary comic, however, and defeated his enemies not with physical prowess but with brain power and positive attitude. In a play called *The Last Dragon of Camelot,* a young woman proved that she had the courage and

EATS FOR KIDS Kids can eat pizza, the specialty, at **Lou Malnati's** (958 W. Wrightwood Ave, tel. 773/832–4030) or choose from items on the children's menu, including spaghetti, lasagna, chicken nuggets, and mini corn dogs. The menu at the **Salt & Pepper Diner** (2575 N. Lincoln Ave., tel. 773/525–8788) includes such kid-friendly food as pancakes, grilled-cheese sandwiches, tater tots, and great milk shakes. Be prepared to wait because the place is often crowded. For fast food, try **McDonald's** (2402 N. Lincoln Ave., tel. 773/388–3621).

Apollo Theater, 2540 N. Lincoln Ave.

 $10 ages 13 and up, $8 children 2-12

 773/529-2690; www.EmeraldCityTheatre.com

Usually Sa 11 and 1:30, Su 1

3-10

know-how to fight and win against a terrifying dragon. Other Emerald City productions, such as the musical *Me Tarzan, You Jane* (about you know who), have turned to Hollywood for inspiration. Kids definitely got into the swing of things theatrical. Frosty the Snowman returns every year during the winter holidays, and fairy tales, such as the Rodgers and Hammerstein adaptation of *Cinderella*, appear regularly as well. Nonsense takes the stage in plays like *Green Eggs and Ham and Other Stories,* based on the works of Dr. Seuss. It was so popular that it ran for a year and a half, though it was never the same from one performance to the next. For the grand finale, kids in the audience got to call out ideas that the actors used to improvise a Seussian-style skit, all done in rhyming dialogue. Pretend play has never been so zany.

HEY, KIDS! Sometimes during a play the actors will want you to join in. If they ask questions, you can shout out the answers. But when the actors are talking to each other, remember to keep quiet so you can hear what they're saying and follow what's happening.

KEEP IN MIND Subscribers get discounts on tickets as well as well-placed reserved seats. Don't worry about being locked into particular dates, because the plan is very flexible. On top of that, your child will receive a birthday card from the company. You don't have to be a subscriber to hold your child's birthday party at the theater, however. Characters from the play even join in the fun. Emerald City also performs several productions a year at Metropolis Performing Arts Centre (111 W. Campbell St., Arlington Heights, tel. 847/577-2121).

ESPN ZONE

B ring along lots of energy when you come to this sporting venue, because it's not just for spectators. It's for athletes big and small, too. No admission is charged to enter this two-story sports bar and entertainment center. You pay based on what you do.

The Sports Arena is the place to play, where everyone can try out their skills. You and your children can dribble and shoot baskets on a half court, scoring points based on the difficulty of the spots from which you shoot. Younger children can show off because the basket can be lowered to suit their stature. Meanwhile you can see how you measure up against the NBA players who have tested the hardwood here. If you prefer, you and your kids can pretend to be NHL players, with one of you taking shots on simulated ice while another plays goalie. Wannabe football players can see if their aim is good enough to throw

KEEP IN MIND Points get used up quickly. Five minutes of baseball costs 15 points, so to maximize your point cards (valid for a year), take some time-outs to watch sporting events. But don't bring youngsters when a popular event is scheduled to air. Overenthusiastic crowds can be overwhelming.

HEY, KIDS! Check out the Zone Art displays, which have been created by local artists. One is made up of thousands of wrappers from Wrigley's chewing gum that have been assembled to create a replica of the Chicago Cubs' Wrigley Field. In a piece called *Oh Say Can You Scream*, a comment on how loudly Blackhawks fans sing the national anthem, hockey sticks and pucks create an American flag. A quilt in honor of the White Sox includes—you guessed it—white socks, as well as baseball cards. How do the cards compare to ones you've collected?

43 E. Ohio St.

 312/644–ESPN;
www.espnzone.com

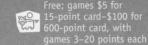 Free; games $5 for
15-point card–$100 for
600-point card, with
games 3–20 points each

M–Th 11:30 AM–12 AM, F–Sa
11:30 AM–12:30 AM, Su 11:30–11:30

 7 and up

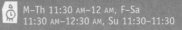

the ball through moving cutouts. And X Games have a place here, too. A simulated rock-climbing wall moves down like a vertical treadmill so you can't get to the top. Don't worry: There's padding all around for those who might lose their footing.

Away from the heaviest action, there are lots of sports-inspired video games, but the Screening Room is the place to really be a couch potato. Here Zone Throne stations have reclining leather chairs where you can watch sporting events on a 16-foot by 13-foot screen.

Kids who feel the urge to take a break don't have to worry about missing out on the action. Even the rest rooms are equipped with television monitors so the play-by-play goes on. After all, first and foremost ESPN is a TV station.

EATS FOR KIDS The **Studio Grill** is decked out like the sets of ESPN shows, including "SportsCenter," "Baseball Tonight," "NBA 2Night," and "NFL Primetime." Nonreaders can still grasp the kids' menu (hamburgers, pizzas, and chicken tenders) by peeking into a View-Master. When the lights dim, a sports report made for ESPN Zone is about to air on more than 200 TVs. And if your children want a memento, you can take their pictures at the SportsCenter desk. Just remember to bring a camera.

FIELD MUSEUM OF NATURAL HISTORY

A brachiosaurus stands at attention outside, letting everyone know that this is dinosaur country. If there was any doubt, the largest, most complete *Tyrannosaurus rex* ever found, the 45-foot-long Sue (named for the woman who discovered it), lurks in the lobby. Dinosaurs also inhabit Life Over Time. Push a button to hear the bellowing sound they might have made, another for their footsteps. If you're brave, push yet another to smell their hypothetical breath. Pause at the Fossil Preparation Lab to see how scientists prepare dino bones. The breadth of the museum's natural history collections go beyond awesome prehistoric creatures, however, and range from the slightly frightening to the enlightening.

Descending through a dim ancient Egyptian tomb can be intimidating, but it's worth it. Mausoleums like this were called the "mansions of eternity" because the deceased who "lived" here were supposed to do so forever. Real mummies are nothing like those that wander around in old movies, though. At the tomb's exit, children can see how Egyptians lived and try to move a stone like the ones in the pyramids.

EATS FOR KIDS The museum's **McDonald's** is decorated with photographs of dinosaur skeletons and fossils and some giant murals of these extinct creatures. You can eat on an outdoor terrace when the weather is nice. A **Corner Bakery,** within a few dinosaur strides of Sue, in the museum's main hall, sells mini sandwiches, muffins, bagels and cream cheese, and even half pizzas. You can also buy box lunches and eat outside on the Museum Campus lawn.

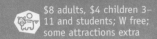 E. Roosevelt Rd. at S. Lake Shore Dr.

 Daily 9–5

$8 adults, $4 children 3–11 and students; W free; some attractions extra

 312/922–9410;
www.fieldmuseum.org

 3 and up

For a firsthand feel for Native Americans of the Great Plains, enter a full-size 19th-century Pawnee Earth Lodge and sit on buffalo robes. Travel to far-off places, including a Pacific islands exhibit where kids can experience a volcano. Into the Wild: Animals, Trails & Tales has realistic dioramas featuring animals in natural settings. Children can push buttons to hear birdsong or play a computer game about controlling the deer population. Young children enjoy What is an Animal?, in which they discover the needs of animals, don goggles to see how a fly sees, and feel the buzz of a replica fish with an electric sensing mechanism. There are creepy, crawly creatures galore in Underground Adventure. Here kids might like being frightened by an animatronic crayfish, earwig, and other soil dwellers. Be prepared; they're as big as a young child. In addition, the museum regularly presents dance, music, and theater productions for all ages as well as story times for youngsters, which get visitors in tune with other cultures and time periods.

KEEP IN MIND
The museum has too many interesting exhibits to be adequately covered in a day by anyone with feet. Get a map and visit the exhibits you really want to see, breaking for food every so often. A free trolley shuttle will get you back to the parking lot.

HEY, KIDS! Look for the Living Together exhibit, which demonstrates the differences and similarities of everyday life in various cultures. A display of some 350 pairs of shoes includes silver wedding slippers from India, snowshoes worn by Eskimos, wooden shoes from the Netherlands, and a pair that belonged to Michael Jordan. They're in a glass case, so you won't be able to hold them up and compare them to your shoes. Trust us: they're bigger.

FRANK LLOYD WRIGHT HOME AND STUDIO

46

What better way to learn about Frank Lloyd Wright's early Prairie-style architecture than to take a guided tour of the house he built for his family in 1889? Though he hadn't fully developed the style, many elements are here.

The best choice for kids is a Junior Interpreter Tour, given by young guides for young people. These focus on the architect's six children and the ways Wright made the home a great place to play. The tour begins by children comparing Victorian and Prairie-style houses. The Victorian is tall, wooden, and has a pointed roof. Wright's house, inspired by the Midwest landscape, is low and flat and made of stucco and bricks. (Surprisingly, though, Wright decorated his house in Victorian fashion for Christmas, as you can see on a free tour offered two Saturdays in December, 9–11.) Then it's time to see the house, whose first three rooms flow together with no doors to separate them.

The playroom is particularly awe inspiring. Here a skylight brings sunshine through the

EATS FOR KIDS At **Peterson's** (715 W. Lake St., tel. 708/848–5020) you can order soup and a sandwich while your children eat dinosaur-shape chicken nuggets or other kids' fare. A sweetshop serves traditional ice-cream treats and the Merry-Go-Round: a chocolate sundae with animal cookies and a parasol.

KEEP IN MIND If Wright's own house has intrigued you, walk around the neighborhood to see other homes he designed. These are marked on a map ($3) available at the shop here. Though these houses are not open to the public, you can look at their facades to get a fuller understanding of Prairie style. The Heurtley House (318 Forest Ave.), built in 1902, is a good example of Wright's strong horizontal lines. The Frank Thomas House (210 Forest Ave.) is also typical Wright. For a fun game, ask your kids if they can pick out his houses.

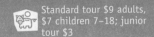
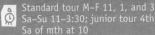

18-foot, barrel-vaulted ceiling. Wright's interest in nature is visible in the leaf and tree decorations in the wooden border around the skylight and in the tulip shapes in the stained-glass windows. A mural depicts "The Fisherman and the Genie," one of the Wright children's favorite stories. Though built-in cabinets create plenty of storage for toys, some are just left out and around. (Some things never change.) In particular, look for the Froebel blocks, which Wright credited with shaping his architectural concepts. The keyboard of a grand piano protrudes from a wall (its back half sticks out on the other side of the wall by a staircase), and the balcony served as stage or gallery, depending on where the children performed.

On to the partitioned bedroom, which Wright's children shared. Though the boys slept on one side and the girls on the other, the wall wasn't high enough to prevent them from having pillow fights over the top. Perhaps your children will see that though the great architect's house is undeniably a work of art, it was also a place where kids not unlike themselves really lived.

HEY, KIDS! To see how Wright *really* incorporated nature in his buildings, check out the enclosed passageway between the home and the studio. Since a tree was already growing here, he simply included it in his plan. The original tree was a weeping willow, but it unfortunately suffered too much stress from the temperature difference resulting from being half indoors and half outdoors. It was replaced in the late '70s with a honey locust, which appears to be holding up.

GARFIELD PARK CONSERVATORY

This large, glass-enclosed conservatory was once a place to look at plants—4 indoor acres of them—but not to touch. That changed in 2000, when the Elizabeth Morse Genius Children's Garden—Plants Alive! opened, welcoming not only hands but bodies, too.

The new exhibit gives an inside look at plants and their life cycle. A giant make-believe vine beckons youngsters to follow its root and make their way to a giant seed, where life begins. Handles all over the seed invite climbing. Children then move along the vine to an enormous leaf—photosynthesis in action. A large pinwheel-like sun shines above, and they can make small yellow balls of "sunshine" fall onto the leaf. The vine continues to the mezzanine, where a giant bee hovers above a flower. Manipulating a pulley brings the insect down to pollinate the flower, and the cycle begins again. To get down from the mezzanine, kids can take the stairs, an elevator, or a slide, which spirals down like a plant tendril. Then it's time for the real thing. Kids can dig in the dirt at the Discovery Area, open drawers with mounted insects, touch and smell plants, or examine leaves on a light table.

KEEP IN MIND The neighborhood around the conservatory isn't very safe, so you shouldn't stray far. Taking a car is your best bet. There's free parking in a lot that's safe for both you and your vehicle, so that shouldn't keep you from visiting. Good reasons to come are the flower shows: the Azalea/Camellia Show (February–March), the Spring Flower Show (early April–mid-May), the Summer Tropical Show (mid-June–early October), Chrysanthemum Flower Show (November), and the Celebration in Lights tropical salute to Santa (mid-December–mid-January).

300 N. Central Park Ave.

 Free

 Daily 9–5

 312/746–5100;
www.garfield-conservatory.org

All ages

Infants have a safe place of their own to explore, surrounded by make-believe fallen logs where parents can sit. While babies play, they're exposed to elements that demonstrate the role of roots, seeds, leaves, and flowers in the life of plants.

Elsewhere in the conservatory, plants from around the world are labeled with interesting information. The Desert House contains cacti, which have adapted to their hot, dry climate, while the Palm House's palms, ficus, and fig trees cope with excess moisture on their leaves. Kids might notice that plants growing close to the ground have big leaves (to get as much sun as possible). Children can imagine dinosaurs devouring the prehistoric plants in the Fern Room and themselves devouring the products of the Warm House's food plants, including banana and cacao trees, both integral to banana splits. Your kids may not have thought about where food comes from before this, but it's amazing what planting a seed in an active mind can do.

HEY, KIDS! Play the Seed Survival Game on an oversize *pachinko* (Japanese-style pinball) machine. If you are lucky, your balls will fall into holes that promise that your seed will receive sunshine, water, and just the right temperature to grow. But beware because, with a bit of bad luck, drought or other bad conditions could prevent your seed from taking root and sprouting.

EATS FOR KIDS
Often on weekends the conservatory has a cart that sells muffins and snacks. The nearest restaurant is **Wishbone** (*see* the Museum of Holography).

GROSSE POINT LIGHTHOUSE

This lighthouse offers up a view of Lake Michigan that will be long remembered, but it's not for everyone. Any individuals who have vertigo, a fear of heights, claustrophobia, or are unsteady on their feet should refrain from a trip up this landmark. Even those in good physical condition may find themselves huffing and puffing on the way up.

A visit begins with a 10-minute film about the history of the lighthouse, which was built in 1873 in response to the shipwreck of the *Lady Elgin*. Nearly 300 people drowned off the Evanston shore. It's not surprising then that in 1908 Charles William Pearson penned a poem that described Grosse Point as "A dreaded point when the north winds roar." Because of its role in maritime commerce between the late 1800s and early 1900s, the lighthouse was named a National Historic Monument in 1999, one of only seven landmark lights in the country. A museum in the keeper's house shows a few historic objects, and a garden is planted with flowers that attract butterflies. But the real attraction here is the lighthouse itself.

HEY, KIDS!
At night you can see the light in action not only from the lake, but also from the west. It flashes 1½ seconds on, 2 seconds off, 1½ seconds on, and 10 seconds off. Try timing it.

EATS FOR KIDS
Bring a blanket and a picnic lunch, and eat in the park just north of the Evanston Art Center, which is next to the lighthouse. A concession truck sometimes visits when the beach behind the art center is open. The simple **Noyes Street Cafe** (828 Noyes St., tel. 847/475–8683) serves some American food as well as Greek specialties. For other options, see the Mitchell Museum of the American Indian.

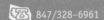 2601 Sheridan Rd., Evanston

 $5 ages 13 and up,
$3 children 8–12

Tours June–Sept, Sa–Su 2, 3, and 4

847/328-6961

8 and up

Pass through a small room with items the keepers used, and begin the climb. The winding cast-iron-grate staircase has steep steps, which get smaller nearer the top. Little windows along the way reveal views of the lake and the adjoining neighborhood, but the best view comes when you crawl into the cramped space with the light or step out onto a narrow walkway. To the east is vast Lake Michigan, to the south the Chicago skyline, and to the north the tree-lined, curving shore of suburban communities.

Legend has it that though the French lens was destined for a southern lighthouse, it was buried in sand during the Civil War and rerouted to Evanston afterward. The first light was provided by an oil lamp, but an electric light was installed in 1922. In fact, the lighthouse is still a beacon for small boats, not to mention adventuresome climbers.

KEEP IN MIND To grade-schoolers, it can seem like a long way up those steep curving stairs. Be ready for some awkward hand holding (you must travel single file) and words of encouragement, if necessary. A few small landings make passing a little easier, but since only 12 people are allowed on the tour at a time, traffic jams don't generally occur. Ask your child to count all 141 steps; it can provide just enough of a distraction to keep complaints to a minimum.

THE GROVE

43

Pioneer Robert Kennicott, known as Illinois's first naturalist, spent his short 30-year life here from 1836 to 1866 and studied the plants and animals that lived alongside him. Today his house and the land around it are a National Historic Landmark. Tours of the home and of a one-room schoolhouse on the property are conducted by guides dressed in 19th-century clothing several times a week between mid-June and mid-August. In an 1860s log cabin, other costumed guides demonstrate the housework of yesteryear: sweeping dirt floors "clean" and scrubbing clothes on a washboard.

But like Kennicott himself, your children will probably be happiest making discoveries about the natural world. A wooden walkway meanders across a pond created by a glacier long, long ago. It's a good place to see floating plants, such as water lilies, and maybe a few turtles and toads, a salamander or two, dragonflies and damselflies, and whirligig beetles that spin on top of the water. In the woods are black willows, some 90 feet tall, whose bark and twigs were used by Native Americans to cure headaches.

KEEP IN MIND Just like their less-pesky animal cousins, mosquitoes like it here. Come with clothes that cover you and, if you must, insect repellent for the wooded trails. Interestingly, you won't find mosquitoes near the buildings. The woods also contain poison ivy, so don't leave the paths.

1421 Milwaukee Ave., Glenview

 Free

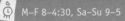 M–F 8–4:30, Sa–Su 9–5

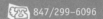 847/299-6096

 4 and up

Children can look closer at some of the wetland's creatures at the large interpretive center, near a Native American teepee and a bark longhouse. Turtles of all sizes move slowly from rock to rock and pull themselves into their shells for a rest in a large aquarium. Look for the alligator snapper, who is about 100 years old. There are also fish and snakes natural to the area. On weekends naturalists offer extra activities, such as puzzles, games, and coloring sheets, focusing on life in the pond or amphibians or bird migration. Annual events, for which there is a small charge, include a Folk Fest, Pumpkin Trail, and Civil War Weekend with costumed soldiers, who fire shots that may be louder than children expect. But even without a special event, the Grove is a wonderful place to visit for a little living history and a lot of living things.

EATS FOR KIDS
Previously allowed, picnics are now discouraged at the Grove, and no food or drink is sold except during special events. A few family-friendly restaurants are nearby, including **Dappers** (4520 W. Lake Ave., tel. 847/699–0020), **T.G.I. Friday's** (4513 W. Lake Ave., tel. 847/298–9966), and **Wendy's** (4610 W. Lake Ave., tel. 847/824–1879).

HEY, KIDS! Once you've developed an eagle eye for spotting birds and other animals in the wild, see if you can find an owl named Mrs. Hoot, who lives in a large cage outdoors. This great horned owl has feathers in various shades of gray, so she blends into her environment very well. And since she's nocturnal—that is, she spends her days sleeping—she'll be very still while you're visiting.

HANCOCK OBSERVATORY

42

Carl Sandburg called Chicago the "Stormy, husky, brawling, City of the Big Shoulders" long before today's skyscrapers muscled their way into the skyline. Fitting right in among its broad-shouldered brethren is the John Hancock Center, dubbed Big John. The tallest building in the world when it was finished in 1970, it is now Chicago's third-tallest, "dwarfed" by the Sears Tower (*see* #8) and the Aon Center. Needless to say there's quite a view from the observatory on the 94th floor.

Your trip to the top begins with a bag search, so travel light. Then it's off to a lower-level area that has been arranged to look like a construction site. A video details the construction of the building, which took four years to complete. Then comes the speedy elevator ride; it takes a little more than 40 seconds and might make your ears pop.

The observatory has a lot to look at within it, but it's the spectacular view outside that will catch your eye first. Walk all the way around to gaze in every direction. To the

KEEP IN MIND There may be a wait—up to a ½ hour—to take the elevator up or down, so plan accordingly. Saturdays are the busiest, Sundays less so. Evenings are also good, especially if you want to see the city in lights. Once at the top, you can stay as long as you like.

EATS FOR KIDS The **Cheesecake Factory** (875 N. Michigan Ave., tel. 312/337–1101) serves more than 30 kinds of cheesecake. Courtyard seating and live music are sometimes offered. Sandwiches at **Chicago Flat Sammies** (811 N. Michigan Ave., tel. 312/664–BRED), in the Pumping Station, which survived the Great Chicago Fire of 1871, are made with bread dough that's flattened before baking. **Foodlife** (835 N. Michigan Ave., Water Tower Place mezzanine level, tel. 312/335–3663) serves wraps, Asian noodles, and sandwiches. The market next door sells takeout.

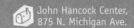 John Hancock Center,
875 N. Michigan Ave.

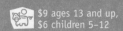 $9 ages 13 and up,
$6 children 5–12

 Daily 9 AM–12 AM

 888/875–VIEW;
www.hancock-observatory.com

 3 and up

east are Lake Michigan and Navy Pier. To the north you can see Oak Street Beach and, on a clear day, even Wisconsin. To the west stretch the United Center (home of the Bulls), O'Hare Airport, expressways, and suburbs as far as the eye can see, and to the south the skyscrapers stand tall. Kids can check out a virtual view of the city with an interactive computer or see the real thing up close while listening to commentary, thanks to a talking telescope. A self-guided audio tour gives snippets of history, humorous details, some blues music, and the sounds of squeegees cleaning the windows. The brave of heart can walk outside (don't worry, it's heavily screened, and there's a sturdy railing) to check out the atmosphere at 1,000 feet above street level. Here they'll discover that even though the Windy City was named for its fast-talking politicians, nature, too, plays its part in Chicago's most famous nickname.

HEY, KIDS! Have your picture taken on a window-washer's scaffolding or while bungee jumping from the top of the building. Well, not really, but the observatory does have sets designed to make your snapshot seem realistic. Or make an e-postcard ($2). A machine equipped with a digital camera not only takes your picture against a Chicago backdrop, but also lets you record a message. Your personalized postcard will then be sent via e-mail.

HAROLD WASHINGTON PLAYLOT PARK

41

Harold Washington, Chicago's first African-American mayor, passed away while still in office in 1987. What better tribute to a man interested in the well-being of children than a playground, and this one is something special. At the entrance is a sculpture of an open book with a relief portrait and quote of Washington's: "I see a Chicago of educational excellence and equality in which all children can learn to function in this ever-more complex society." Since children learn about the world through play, this is the perfect place to continue their education.

The park's centerpiece is a big wooden red, white, and black ship that seems to be waiting for children to climb aboard and take imaginary journeys. It "floats" on a soft blue rubberized surface that doesn't hurt the occasional "kid overboard." A wooden castle encourages another whole set of make-believe games. Metal equipment in cheerful primary colors is divided into two areas. One has spring-based dinosaur riders, baby swings, ladders,

EATS FOR KIDS The park is the perfect place for a picnic, thanks to green grass all around and a lakefront setting with a splendid view of the city in the background. The **Dixie Kitchen and Bake Shop** (5225 S. Harper Ave., tel. 773/363–4943) has Cajun food and grilled-cheese sandwiches, hamburgers, and chicken nuggets. **Calypso Cafe** (5211 S. Harper Ave., tel. 773/955–0229) has Caribbean cuisine for adults and a kids' menu with pizza, chicken nuggets, and other American favorites. Familiar fare can be found at **Mc-Donald's** (1344 E. 53rd St., tel. 773/493–1622) and **Boston Market** (1424 E. 53rd St., tel. 773/288–2600).

Hyde Park Blvd. from 51st to 53rd Sts.

 Free

 Daily 6 AM–11 PM

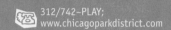 312/742–PLAY;
www.chicagoparkdistrict.com

 2–12

and bridges that are all just the right size for younger children. The other is designed to challenge the physical prowess of older kids, who clamber over monkey bars, tire swings, tunnels, rings, ladders, and slides, including one that's wide enough for two. A sandbox with sloped edges might actually get toddlers to sit for a while, and two spray pools with soft surfaces keep both big and little ones cool when the weather gets hot. In one, water sprays into the air as well as out of the mouths of sea horses.

There are plenty of benches for parents to sit, relax, and supervise, and since the playground is surrounded by a low-level wrought-iron fence with only one exit, children aren't likely to escape without you. The two-block-long park around the playground is grass covered and has plenty of tall, shady trees and enough open space to play Frisbee.

HEY, KIDS! If you're a triker, ride your three-wheeler on a path just for you (no bikes allowed). Running all around the playground (don't worry: you can always see your parents), the path is also made for wheelchairs. Spray pools and the ship are accessible, too.

KEEP IN MIND Packing for the playground has never been so complicated. If the weather is nice and hot, remember to bring towels to dry your children off after a spray pool session. A swimsuit is a good idea, too. Kids can change in the rest rooms. If the weather is even a little cool, bring an extra layer of warm clothes. Since the park is right across from the lake, it can be colder here than where you came from. The park has drinking fountains and an occasional ice-cream truck but no place to buy other food, so come prepared.

40

Kids may think that health and fun don't go together, but the more than 200 hands-on activities in this three-level museum will prove them wrong. Here children can discover how to keep themselves and the planet healthy while indeed having a good time.

Even big kids are bowled over by Kelly, nicknamed the Big Kid, who seems to be bowled over, too. An 85-foot-long fiberglass girl in a Little League uniform is stretched out on the floor near the entrance. Even reclining on her back she is two stories tall. Kids can walk inside and discover the details of human anatomy, crawling through her heart if they wish. In her backpack, also known as the Brain Theater, they can see a multimedia presentation, showing how a child's body reacts on a typical day. For example, when Kelly falls off her bike, they'll see what happens in her ear when she loses her balance.

Children can learn what good foods to choose in a grocery store area. They can watch a puppet show about germs and examine the concept firsthand by washing their hands

KEEP IN MIND If you and your child are ready for it, head to Life Trek, which uses video games to explain where babies come from and how life ends. You'll want to stay close at hand to guide your child through and be prepared for discussions afterward.

HEY, KIDS! Near Kelly, some gadgets—even good for 4-year-olds—let you test your strength and coordination. Squeeze a lever and watch a numbered scale light up, measuring your strength. See how long you can hang from a horizontal bar and how high you can jump. Listen for the sound that reveals how high you leaped. The higher the jump, the higher the pitch. There are enough gadgets to go around, so you won't have to wait too long for a turn.

1301 S. Grove Ave., Barrington

 F 10–8, Sa–Th 10–3

 $5 ages 2 and up

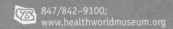 847/842-9100;
www.healthworldmuseum.org

 4–13

with Glow Germ lotion and looking at them under ultraviolet light to see if any germs remain. It might even lead to more energetic hand washing.

Kids can discover potential dangers in your house, practice escaping a fire, and dial 911 to hear a realistic message. They can check their knowledge of bike safety by pedaling through a virtual village and feel what it's like to ride uphill and downhill with the wind blowing. Elsewhere they can test their reaction time when a traffic light changes and discover that air bags inflate in the blink of an eye. They can also pretend to be a doctor, dressing in scrubs, performing pretend surgery, and using instruments to diagnose problems. There is a place to test hearing, to find out what doctors see when they examine ears, and to fill a cavity in an oversize tooth. To find out about the health of the environment, your children can climb into Pete's Treehouse and Joey's Ranger Station. A visit to the museum is not only enlightening; it's good, clean, healthy fun.

EATS FOR KIDS The museum's **Georgi's Garden Cafe** has child-friendly food, including turkey sandwiches, Italian beef sandwiches, pizza, and chicken tenders. The dessert menu offers fresh-baked cookies and, as befits the museum's mission, such healthy choices as fruit cups and applesauce. Weather permitting, hot dogs and hamburgers are cooked on the barbecue outside.

Journey to America's past while riding the rails at this 120-acre museum. It all started in 1941, when a group of rail buffs purchased a high-speed electric railroad car that was bound for oblivion. But they didn't stop there. Eventually, their collection grew so large that, in 1964, they purchased a 26-acre farm for a museum. Today some 400 engines and cars have been, or are being, restored by volunteers, who also don uniforms and operate some of them.

Step inside a 1923 baggage car to buy your ticket, good for unlimited rides. While waiting, you can sit in an authentic 1851 station and peer through ticket windows at railroad memorabilia. However, the real thrill comes when you climb aboard the trains at the platform outside. There's never a long wait because cars are added as needed.

Your engine might be 200 tons of steam locomotive. Standing 15 feet tall with hissing brakes and bellowing steam, it's the mechanical equivalent of a dinosaur as it puffs out

EATS FOR KIDS A **concession stand** sells hot dogs, nachos, sweets, and drinks, which can be enjoyed at picnic tables. Also on the grounds, an old-fashioned casual sit-down **restaurant** has been added onto a refurbished 1930s trackside diner, part of a chain called **Jerry O'Mahony.**

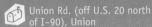 Union Rd. (off U.S. 20 north of I-90), Union

 800/BIG-RAIL; www.irm.org

M–F $6 ages 12 and up, $4 children 5–11; regular Sa–Su $8 ages 12 and up, $6 children; steam/diesel Sa–Su $9 ages 12 and up, $7 children

 Grounds Apr–Oct, daily 9–6; trains Apr, Su 10:30–5, May–Oct, Sa–Su 10:30–5, also Memorial Day–Labor Day, M–F 10–4

 3 and up

of the station. An Electroliner, which ran between Chicago and Milwaukee until 1963 and is powered by overhead wires, sways back and forth, sometimes giving a little lurch as it clickety-clacks down the tracks. Several 1950s diesel trains come along, too. Although the electrics and diesels once sped up to 80 mph, for safety's sake, they only reach 30–40 mph today. But even that seems fast as they travel through a landscape of corn fields and old farmhouses and barns. Days when each type of train operates vary: Electric cars run every day. Diesels operate most weekends and holidays May–September, and steam trains chug about a dozen times each season. In addition, on some days a streetcar takes you to nine gigantic barns with everything from luxurious, turn-of-the-20th-century private passenger cars to red cabooses to the streamlined 1930s silver Zephyr. Special events include a July 4 trolley parade, Civil War day, and a visit by Thomas the Tank Engine. In time the museum plans to buy its own big-eyed, blue engine. All aboard!

HEY, KIDS! Hop on the small open yellow section car, which sits without moving on a small track. It's called Speeder, but it didn't go very fast because it didn't have a motor. Workers responsible for maintaining the tracks used to operate it by pumping a lever.

KEEP IN MIND Take the time to read the museum rules to your children, since trains can be dangerous. Among other things, it's important to stop, look, and listen for trains coming on the tracks. Overhead trolley wires, which carry 600 volts of electricity, and any poles and objects touching them can cause electrocution.

INDIAN BOUNDARY PARK

38

Sometimes a neighborhood park is more than just a neighborhood park. This one has a little something extra. The playground contains a vast wooden structure with places to swing and slide, climb and hide, and a log locomotive for make-believe getaways. A spray pool is ideal on hot summer days (mid-June–Labor Day). It's like running through the jet from an opened fire hydrant, only legal. And a Tudor-style field house, built in 1929, has art and ornamentation inspired by Native American culture, since the site was once a territorial boundary between Potowatomi Indian and U.S. government land—hence the name Indian Boundary.

The park also has a miniature zoo, which started in the 1920s when someone donated a bear. It was almost shut down years ago, but a community outcry kept it open. Managed by the Lincoln Park Zoo, the zoolet has a white-tailed deer; some domestic goats, raised for milk; a pigmy goat from Africa; an alpaca; and a mute swan. Incidentally, in 12th-century England, mute swans were considered so extraordinary that only members of

HEY, KIDS!
The alpaca in the zoo is from a family of South American mammals that includes the llama, which is primarily a pack animal. The alpaca, however, is raised for its wool, but unfortunately you're not allowed to touch its coat here.

KEEP IN MIND If it's a warm day, remember to bring swimsuits and towels so your kids will be able to play in the spray pool and dry off afterwards. Lamentably, there's no parking lot, so you'll have to search for a spot on the street and walk. If you want more activity than a stroll to the car, you can walk to nearby Warren Park, which has batting cages and an outdoor track designed for in-line skating that becomes a skating rink in the winter.

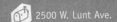 2500 W. Lunt Ave.

 312/742-7887;
www.chicagoparkdistrict.com

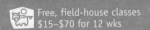 Free, field-house classes
$15–$70 for 12 wks

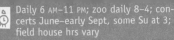 Daily 6 AM–11 PM; zoo daily 8–4; concerts June–early Sept, some Su at 3; field house hrs vary

 All ages

royalty were allowed to own them. Your children mustn't try to feed the animals. They have their own specific diets to keep them healthy and must be hungry enough at closing time to want the treats they're given to lure them inside.

Next to the zoo, an exhibit area has houses to attract birds and bats and vegetation to attract butterflies. A lagoon with a geyser in the middle brings wild ducks and Canada geese. Please don't feed these animals either; it would attract too many birds, and the lagoon would become overpopulated. The park also has many grassy areas and trees, so though there isn't a spot for baseball or basketball, there's room to throw a Frisbee. Surprisingly, the field house is the venue for the arts rather than sports. Classes in art, dance, and drama are offered throughout the year, as are public performances.

In summer, free Sunday afternoon concerts feature musical fare from salsa to the blues to classical. It's a fitting end to a full, rich day in the park.

EATS FOR KIDS Pack your own picnic. You won't be alone. Neighborhood residents bring food that reflects their many different ethnic backgrounds and often eat it while listening to the music of their particular culture. Barbecuing is allowed on hip-high grills only. For dessert, you can count on ice-cream trucks coming regularly throughout the day.

INTERNATIONAL MUSEUM OF SURGICAL SCIENCE

The first sign of what's to come is out front: a sculpture of a doctor holding a limp patient, called *Hope and Help*. The faint of heart or stomach may want to skip this museum, but others will be fascinated by its large collection of historical objects designed for healing, many more imaginative than effective. The museum is housed in a 1917 mansion inspired by a French château on the property of Versailles, but though the building is elegant, its four floors of exhibits tend to the creepy. And except for one button in the drugstore, which you can push to hear about a pharmacist's profession around 1900, the museum is a traditional one where you look but don't touch.

Among the exhibits are bright-colored handmade objects the Aztecs used to rid people of various ills and 4,000-year-old skulls from Peru with holes bored into them so that evil spirits could escape. Skull boring was also used more recently to cure blindness and insanity. (A skeleton in a classroom setting shows how surgeons finally learned about human anatomy—thank goodness.) Civil War objects include some bullets and an amputation kit,

KEEP IN MIND The museum has changing art exhibits with works inspired by the human body. Though some of them are abstract paintings or photographs, others are realistic portrayals—perhaps of cadavers or images of scars and sutures—and so may be disturbing. Be prepared to talk with your children about the works and the emotions they evoke. This is also a good opportunity to discuss how important it is for artists to be able to express their feelings about the human body, illness, and death in their work.

 1524 N. Lake Shore Dr.

 $2 suggested donation; T free

T-Sa 10-4

312/642-6502; www.imss.org

 10 and up

and a mural—one of many throughout the museum depicting surgery—graphically shows a man writhing in pain during an amputation. An old-fashioned drugstore has jars and bottles and boxes of various concoctions. As preposterous as it sounds, there are even special cigarettes that were supposed to help people with bronchitis. A re-created turn-of-the-20th-century physician's office contains tools ready and waiting to deliver babies, remove abscesses or lumps, or even bleed patients with colds or insomnia. There is also a room with early X-ray equipment as well as a 1950s Buster Brown Shoe Fitter, which unbelievably used X rays to check the fit of new shoes. It was around this time that scientists began to realize that doses of radiation could be harmful.

Don't be surprised if your children come away wondering how sick people ever survived all these treatments, let alone the illnesses, and thankful to live today rather than in olden times.

> **EATS FOR KIDS**
> At the **Big Bowl** (6 E. Cedar St., tel. 312/640-8888), an Asian noodle shop, kids eat Chinese crunchy chicken sticks, satay, potstickers, barbecued chicken, or egg noodles with easy-to-use chopsticks. The **Corner Bakery** (1121 N. State St., tel. 312/787-1969) makes salads, sandwiches, pasta, and pizza.

HEY, KIDS! Play the first-floor Germ Find game and learn about germs—like how doctors didn't know about them before 1850. Look at a photo of a pre-germ theory operation. Would you want to be operated on by surgeons without gloves or masks, while paying spectators watch, the way they once did?

JOHN G. SHEDD AQUARIUM

36

More than 70% of the earth is covered with water, remaining largely hidden from us. But not at this dual facility, which includes the world's largest indoor aquarium, housed in a 1930 Greek-style building, and the attached white-marble indoor oceanarium (1991), which overlooks Lake Michigan and features marine mammals. Together they contain more than 8,000 animals from the world's oceans, rivers, and lakes.

At the oceanarium, you can stroll through re-created habitats reflecting the Pacific coastline from Northern California to Alaska's Prince William Sound. Shows four or five times a day let the mammals show off natural behaviors: Pacific white-sided dolphins leap, walk on their tails, and breach (jumping and slapping their bodies against the water). Beluga whales spin, flap their fins, and wave their tails. A "nature trail" leads to seals and sea otters. They're great fun to watch, as are the graceful creatures in the Seahorse Symphony and the penguins (exceptions to the mammals-only policy), especially from the Underwater Viewing Gallery. Hands-on activities teach about marine mammals.

KEEP IN MIND Come dressed for a trip through the world's climatic zones. The oceanarium is kept chilly for the sake of the animals' health, while temperatures reach tropical levels in Amazon Rising. Sounds of rain and flashes of lightning signal the flood season, but you won't get wet.

HEY, KIDS! The aquarium and oceanarium are home to several animals and ecosystems that are endangered: the Tahitian land snail; the South American bonytongue (a fish that people along the Amazon River eat); the African cichlid; the sea otter; various sea turtles; the Cayman Island rock iguana (that lizard with spines on its back); and coral reefs, which are threatened by global warming, human collectors, ship anchors, and runoff from land. See if you can find them all.

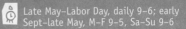

In the aquarium, Amazon Rising: Seasons of the River is an amazing trek through a rain forest that shows how everyone adjusts to the river's ebb and flow. Among the more than 250 mammals, insects, fish, reptiles, amphibians, and birds, you might see a fish called a water monkey, named for its ability to leap out of the floodwaters to catch beetles and spiders, or the lily trotter bird, which can walk on water. You'll have to look closely because most Amazon creatures are well camouflaged. A journey to Philippine coral reefs is expected in early 2003.

Elsewhere in the aquarium, weird and wonderful fish are displayed in darkened galleries so you feel like you're underwater, too. The most popular spot is the Caribbean Reef at feeding time. A diver in the 90,000-gallon tank describes the creatures and their diet. No, the big ones won't eat the little ones. A tank within a tank separates them. Try to find green moray eels (up to 6 feet long) or nurse sharks, both excellent hiders. You can't miss the barracuda, though, with its long pointed jaw and torpedo-shape body.

EATS FOR KIDS The aquarium has a cafeteria-style restaurant called the **Bubble Net** (tel. 312/692–3277), which looks over Lake Michigan. It offers Pizza Hut pizza, hamburgers, hot dogs, chicken fingers, sandwiches, and salads. **Soundings** (tel. 312/692–3277), a sit-down restaurant that also has lake views, serves more sophisticated food for adults as well as children's fare: peanut butter and jelly sandwiches served with fruit, spaghetti, and chicken fingers and fries.

KOHL CHILDREN'S MUSEUM

Though this two-story museum is enjoyed by infants through young grade-schoolers, even adults rediscover their inner child at this quintessential kindergarten. It's a nurturing place where kids play to their heart's content without realizing they're learning.

Research has shown the beneficial effects of music on the development of young brains. The Music Makers exhibit is the place to put theory into practice. Children can create music by sending balls through a giant Rube Goldberg–type contraption called the Sensational Sound Sculpture. They can also put musical notes on the lines of a staff and play their composition back on a variety of instruments, create a collage of music and color, and discover the soothing sounds and raucous tunes that little hands and minds can imagine. For nutritional sustenance, kids can go on a shopping spree in the museum's miniature supermarket, after which they can take a break in the store's replica café. But nobody rests for long because there's too much to do.

EATS FOR KIDS Everybody loves **Walker Bros. Original Pancake House** (153 Green Bay Rd., tel. 847/251–6000), especially on Sunday mornings (it's crowded). Kids love the silver-dollar pancakes: chocolate chip, blueberry, or plain. At **Panera Bread** (1199 Wilmette Ave., tel. 847/853–8170) children can get sandwiches, soup, and chocolate-chip cookies or muffins. Take home a loaf of bread. **Homer's Restaurant & Ice Cream Parlor** (1237 Green Bay Rd., tel. 847/251–0477) serves meals, but the star is the ice cream.

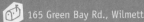 165 Green Bay Rd., Wilmette

 $5 ages 1 and up

 M 9–12, Tu–Sa 9–5, Su 12–5; discovery programs M 10:30–11:30, Tu–Sa 10:30–11:30 and 3–4, Su 3–4

847/251–7781;
www.kohlchildrensmuseum.org

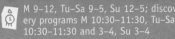 0–8

In the Construction Zone, kids don hard hats, erect a child-size house using bricks and tiles, and landscape it with soft-sculpture flowers. In the StarMax Technology Center, software helps with reading, math, or art, along with being fun. At the H_2O exhibit, everything gets wet except the kids, who wear waterproof aprons. Next it's on to the hospital nursery, with baby dolls in many colors, all waiting to be cuddled. Real babies have their own discovery space in the Cozy Corner, where they can watch mobiles or themselves (in mirrors). Those who can move on their own can crawl over soft shapes and pull themselves up on cruising bars.

Some exhibits are permanent, while some change. Discovery programs offer hands-on activities—from celebrating Elvis Presley's birthday to making sundials to painting with sponges. The museum's motto is "I hear and I forget, I see and I remember, I touch and I understand." Everywhere here, you see little hands busy touching and understanding.

KEEP IN MIND In some places here, kids play on their own; in others, you can and should play with them. Follow your kids' lead and watch what other people are doing. By both interacting and observing, you can enjoy your children's discoveries even more—and so can they.

HEY, KIDS! Check out the activity in the People exhibit that's called Beautiful People; it demonstrates that beautiful people come in all colors. When you dance to music in a darkened space here, your silhouette is projected larger than life on a big screen and constantly changes colors. Each one is as extraordinary as the one before, as are other people's silhouettes, also in ever-changing colors. Try to get your parents to try it, too. Groovy.

THE L

A lot of cities have subways, but Chicago has an elevated train known as the L. A trip around the Loop—originally named for the cable cars that circled this business and shopping district and still encircled by the 1897 L tracks—and out into a residential neighborhood is a great way to see the city. The trains screech and groan, but they keep on traveling, giving you a close-up, second-story view in some parts and a ground-level or underground peek in others.

The L has several different lines. A good excursion follows the Brown Line from the Merchandise Mart south for a trip around the Loop and then north out of the city center to the terminal at Kimball. Crossing the Chicago River, your children can see the city's bridges and boats traveling to and from Lake Michigan. At Wells and Lake streets, the L meets up with lines going in various directions. This was the world's busiest intersection in the 1930s, when a train came through every 20 seconds. As the train continues, urge your kids to look for signs of preservation and growth: scaffolding on old buildings being renovated and heavy

HEY, KIDS!
Ask a parent to point out the corner of State and Lake streets, where a humorous parking garage designed by architect Stanley Tigerman sits. The awning looks like car tires, and the facade resembles a Rolls-Royce's grille. Its turquoise color was used on 1957 Chevrolets.

KEEP IN MIND Don't lecture your kids on architectural history during the ride. Chances are they won't remember it, and the train won't stop long enough. The only date to mention is 1871, when fire destroyed Chicago, which was then rebuilt from the bottom up . . . and up and up. This trip is best seen as an opportunity for kids to observe the urban landscape, so they can gradually appreciate architecture and urban planning. For more, the Chicago Architecture Foundation (224 S. Michigan Ave., tel. 312/922–3432) has a book for families called *Look Up* and also gives Loop train tours.

 The Loop; suggested entrance Merchandise
Mart, Wells St. south of Kinzie St.

 $1.50 ages 12 and up,
75¢ children 7–11

Brown Line M–Sa 5 AM–12 AM, Su 7:15
AM–12 AM; different hrs for other lines

312/836–7000;
www.transitchicago.com

6 and up

equipment where new ones are being built. Buildings built in 1871, right after the Great Chicago Fire, are easy to recognize, because they're only four or five stories high, the limit people would climb before the advent of passenger elevators. They also have tall, skinny windows.

As the train turns onto Van Buren Street, watch for the white terra-cotta Insurance Exchange Building, built between 1914 and 1928. One of its corners looks like it was cut off, but it was designed that way so the train wouldn't hit it.

The train continues through the city past many interesting structures and ways of life, finally recrossing the Chicago River, coming down to ground level, and skirting people's backyards. To return downtown, you can board another train at Kimball without paying a second fare, but you might want to change at Fullerton to the Red Line, which stops along State Street. The Red goes underground, making it seem like a theme park ride, only gentler.

EATS FOR KIDS If you take the Red Line to return, you can get off at Chicago Avenue and State Street (*see* Hancock Observatory for eateries). If you get off at Grand Avenue and State Street, you'll be near many theme restaurants: **Ed Debevic's Short Order Deluxe** (640 N. Wells St., tel. 312/664–1707), the **Hard Rock Cafe** (63 W. Ontario St., tel. 312/943–2252), **Rock 'n' Roll McDonald's** (600 N. Clark St., tel. 312/664–7940), and the **Rainforest Cafe** (605 N. Clark St., tel. 312/787–1501).

LAKEFRONT BIKE WAY

Fitness and fun go together along this 18½-mile bicycle path that follows the beautiful shoreline of Lake Michigan. You can spend a pleasant day just riding along the lake with your family, perhaps pausing for a picnic, or you can stop at any of the many museums and other cultural and recreational attractions along the way.

The parks and beaches all along the bikeway have metered parking spots, so you can start at any point and explore the lakefront bit by bit. If you want to pedal the bike trail's southern end, park at Promontory Point (55th St. and the lake), where there is a beautiful view of the city and nearby Harold Washington Playlot Park (see #41). From here you can ride toward the Museum of Science and Industry (see #22) and the Japanese-style Osaka Garden in Jackson Park.

Another option is to park along Columbus Drive between Monroe and Jackson drives and then head east toward the lake to find the bike path. This gives you the option of riding

KEEP IN MIND The path can be crowded with cyclists, in-line skaters, runners, and walkers, so make sure your children know the rules of the road: Stay to the right, between the center yellow line and the white warning lines, and let faster travelers pass. Watch for "zebra stripes," which warn of upcoming intersections, and three yellow stripes at path entrances, which mean bikes aren't allowed. To stop, move off the bikeway. Call the Chicago Park District for a bikeway map or for details on Bike Chicago (mid-May–mid-June), which includes bike parades, bike art projects, and other activities at city parks.

Parallel to Lake Shore Dr.,
between Hollywood Ave. and 71st St.

 Free

 Daily 6 AM–11 PM

312742–PLAY Chicago Park District;
www.chicagoparkdistrict.com

8 and up

south or north. If you go south, you'll pass by all the boats in Monroe Harbor, to the east of Grant Park, and on to the park's Buckingham Fountain (Lake Shore Dr. south of Jackson Dr.), which was built in 1927 and inspired by a fountain at Versailles. Farther south is the city's triumvirate of museums—the Adler Planetarium and Astronomy Museum, the Field Museum of Natural History, and the John G. Shedd Aquarium (*see* listings)—surrounded by the park area known as the Museum Campus. If you go north from Grant Park, you'll pass by Oak Street Beach, one of Chicago's most popular, and on to the Lincoln Park Zoo. You'll pass a replica of a Haidan Indian totem pole and Montrose Harbor, all the while watching people having picnics; playing baseball, soccer, and basketball; flying kites; and, like you, having a good time.

EATS FOR KIDS

There are concession stands and cafés all along the bikeway. Two good places to stop are the Lincoln Park Zoo (*see* #29) and Buckingham Fountain. Of course, there are also plenty of places to picnic. For even more options, *see* North Avenue Beach.

HEY, KIDS! Don't forget to wear your helmet. Experts say that to be really safe, it should be level on your head, not tilted either forward or back. If your helmet's on right, you should be able to look up and see its front edge.

LATTOF YMCA

E veryone in the family can have fun at the Lattof YMCA. It has the usual activities you'd expect at a Y—cardiovascular- and weight-training areas, an indoor running track, nine handball/racquetball courts, an aerobics room, and three indoor pools—but there's also a lot more, all available with a guest pass.

A triple-decker play area called 'Mazing Kids makes children happy while they're working on their large-motor skills. They can crawl through tubes, climb on nets and webs, try out mini slides, or jump around joyously in a pit of brightly colored balls. Children under 5 need adult supervision, but that can be fun, too, since you can join them.

Older children can romp on their own or take part in Generation X-type sports while you engage in other activities in the facility. While you work out on exercise bicycles, they can work on their gravity-defying tricks at the skate park, as long as you sign a waiver and the weather permits. Possessing just the right surface for skateboarding, the park

HEY, KIDS!
If you get good grades, you can score a second time at the Y. Just bring in your report card at the end of each marking period. Each A you receive earns you one chance in the A TEAM raffle for cool skating stuff.

EATS FOR KIDS Vending machines dispense sandwiches, soup, and snacks, which you can eat at tables by the pool, or bring your own food. At the **Choo Choo** (600 Lee St., tel. 847/391–9815), an authentic '50s diner, a small locomotive chugs around the restaurant delivering hamburgers, hot dogs, and french fries in baskets perched on its flat cars. Kids can watch real trains going by while eating breakfast or lunch at the **L & L Restaurant** (456 Northwest Hwy., tel. 847/803–6767). The **Sugar Bowl** (1494 Miner St., tel. 847/824–7380) has pancakes decorated like a well-known mouse, hamburgers, and other kid-friendly food.

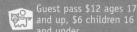
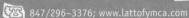
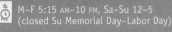

has a half-pipe, rails, and everything else needed to master the techniques of this sport. You may not want to watch, but you'll be happy to know that helmets and wrist guards are required and that knee and elbow pads are highly recommended. Lattof also offers in-line skating and skateboard lessons.

Also in the extreme vein, the Y offers courses in climbing; upon completion, your children can use the 25-foot climbing wall. For a different kind of climbing, your young adventurers can make their way through a constructed indoor cave with hand- and footholds or tackle a high-ropes course. Its 17 elements include the Burma Bridge, the Kitten Crawl, Earthquake Tremor, and the Floating Bridge, all suspended in air. Classes, which teach the intricacies of various techniques, are a must. All in all, your young daredevils can get their fill of extreme sports, while you can try hard not to worry. After a day of X games at the Y, you'll all be ready for some Z's.

KEEP IN MIND Remember that no two children are alike. Some will love the physical challenges in store here, while others may be fearful. A little coaxing can do the trick, but in some cases, pushing a child who isn't ready is counterproductive. The goal should be to have fun, and increased self-confidence is often the by-product.

LET'S DRESS UP

Parents are always telling their kids they can be anything they want to be when they grow up. But why wait? At Let's Dress Up, your children can try on their dreams now. All they need is a fertile imagination and the right clothes. And the choice of clothes here—elaborate kid-size costumes with realistic details—is plenty large.

Kids can choose between total fantasy and quasi-reality, between good guys and bad guys. Although boys tend to be the ones to transform themselves into knights, dragons, and cowboys, and girls gravitate to fairy-tale princesses and the like, both genders can suit up in whatever suits their fancies. Children can take their inspiration from *Star Wars*, dressing as C3PO or Darth Vader, or from MTV, wearing outfits made from as much glitter as spandex. Girls (or boys with a good sense of style and/or humor) might opt for a bridal gown with a bouffant skirt, layers of lace, and a cathedral train or one with elegant satin and a beaded bodice. From the ridiculous to the sublime and back again they all go, putting together perfectly coordinated outfits or mixing and matching as the mood strikes.

EATS FOR KIDS Lombard has plenty of familiar if uninspiring fast-food chains: **Boston Market** (150 E. Roosevelt Rd., tel. 630/620–0400), **Burger King** (401 E. Roosevelt Rd., tel. 630/916–9499), **McDonald's** (300 E. Roosevelt Rd., tel. 630/620–4280), and **Wendy's** (820 E. Roosevelt Rd., tel. 630/495–2730). In nearby Villa Park, **Kappy's** (10 E. Roosevelt Rd., tel. 630/530–4600) has hamburgers, fried chicken, and macaroni and cheese, as well as pancakes that look like a famous mouse, which are also on the menu at **Lumes Pancake House** (180 E. Roosevelt Rd., tel. 630/530–5426) along with silver-dollar pancakes, chocolate-chip pancakes, and hamburgers, too.

1222 S. Highland Ave., Lombard

 $6 1 hr, $8 1½ hrs children 13 and under; tea party $1.25

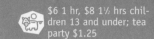 M–Sa 11–6, Su 12–5

630/932-7529

3–13

Make-believe doesn't stop with the right wardrobe. Rooms are decorated as matching settings, such as a ballroom fit for princes and princesses and a rustic-style room out of the Old West for cowboys and cowgirls. An enchanted forest is the place where kids hopping around in bunny costumes may come face to face with ones prowling around like fierce tigers, but it's also a small world where fairy tales have happy endings. However, to really make sure that your endings, not to mention your beginnings, will be happy, you'll want to call ahead for reservations.

HEY, KIDS! Ask your parents if you can stay for the hourly tea party. You can keep your costume on while you drink lemonade and eat cookies, pretzels, or other tasty snacks. Teatime also includes glitter nails and makeup for girls and tattoos and face painting for boys.

KEEP IN MIND Let's Dress Up has similar costumes for adults, too, so feel free to join in the fun. But try to let your children call the shots; remember this is make-believe. Because there are no dressing rooms, your kids should come wearing clothes that aren't too bulky—such as shorts and a T-shirt or a leotard—so that the costumes will fit nicely over them.

LIFELINE THEATRE KIDSERIES

Lifeline Theatre is an award-winning professional theater company known for its creative stage adaptations of such literary works as *Jane Eyre*. What this ensemble of 17 adapters, composers, actors, directors, designers, and visual artists does for grown-ups, it also does for children.

KidSeries plays are original adaptations of favorite children's books and often include charming music written especially for them. The same high standards and originality apply equally to these productions, which are presented in the company's cozy 100-seat theater. Though the plays for young people are thoroughly professional, they have a feeling of innocence and spontaneity, whimsy and quirkiness—almost as if they were put on by children in their own backyard.

Take, for example, a musical adaptation of Mary Jane Auch's *Hen Lake,* about a chicken named Poulette who wants to be a ballet star. In the production, Poulette wore a big

HEY, KIDS!
Head to the lobby and its comfy oversize chair from a production of *Bunnicula*. You'll have to climb up into it or get a boost, and only two people are allowed in it at a time. Why don't you share your turn with your sibling or parent?

KEEP IN MIND Though the neighborhood is on the upswing, it still looks a bit run-down, but never fear. Families have been coming to this theater safely and happily for years. Nevertheless, you wouldn't want to linger long or roam the streets, where sidewalks are littered and loitering is common. You shouldn't have any problem finding metered parking on Morse Avenue. Theater patrons also can find free parking three blocks directly north of the theater at the corner of Glenwood and Estes avenues in the Trilogy, Inc. lot.

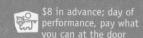 6912 N. Glenwood Ave.

 Usually Sa–Su 1

 773/761–4477;
www.lifelinetheatre.com

$8 in advance; day of
performance, pay what
you can at the door

 4 and up

tutu over her fluffy feathers and striped leg warmers, and her rival, Percival the peacock, wore a coat of many colors and spoke with a preponderance of words starting with the letter "p." Songs ranged from a bebop number sung by pigeons (played by puppets) and a sweet number sung by Poulette about making her dreams come true to a concerto-like piece accompanying her triumphant dance performance. In *The Silver Chair,* puppets and actors with and without masks joined forces in an adaptation of the book by C.S. Lewis.

After each performance, actors come out to the lobby to meet kids, give autographs, and answer questions. So it should come as no surprise that the theater has a faithful following, many of whom expressed their spirit by coming to a presentation of *101 Dalmatians* bedecked in black spots on a white background. But no matter what the play, your children will undoubtedly enjoy its imaginativeness, humor, and warmheartedness and come away feeling that all is right with the world, and so will you.

EATS FOR KIDS Some people think that the **Heartland Cafe** (7000 N. Glenwood Ave., tel. 773/465–8005), which opened in the mid-'70s and has kept that era's ambience, is a vegetarian restaurant, but this popular place also serves chicken and fish. Macaroni and cheese and peanut butter and jelly sandwiches are always available on request. **Leona's** (6935 N. Sheridan Rd., tel. 773/764–5757) is part of a family-run chain that offers small pizzas, chicken strips, and spaghetti on the kids' menu.

LINCOLN PARK ZOO

Like many other zoos, this one showcases animals in settings resembling their natural habitats. What sets it apart are its manageable size and its free admission, both of which make it easy to see what you want and leave before anyone gets exhausted. Pick up a free visitor guide from the Information Center at the east entrance, and decide what to see first. Among the primates, a howler monkey, whose call can be heard miles away, and some acrobatic white-cheeked gibbons swing from branch to branch in a rain-forest environment. The Small Mammal–Reptile House contains environments from four continents. Look closely to find snakes, sloths, and spiders hidden in the vegetation.

For an underwater adventure, take the underground passageway at the Sea Lion Pool to see sea lions and seals. The bird house contains exotic birds, though penguins and seabirds live elsewhere. Kids can see tigers, lions, and cheetahs, but if they want aardvarks, ostriches, giraffes, rhinos, elephants, gorillas, and chimpanzees, they'll have to be patient. These animals have been sent to other zoos while the African Journey landscape is being

EATS FOR KIDS The **Landmark Cafe** sells hot dogs, fries, and snacks. **Cafe Brauer**, in a historic Prairie-style building overlooking a pond, serves standard fare. Kids munch animal-shape fries (and other food-court options) in animal-shape chairs in the **Park Place Cafe.** The rooftop **Big Cats Cafe,** overlooking the birds of prey, lions, and Lake Michigan, offers sandwiches on various breads. Some people eat at **R.J. Grunts** (2056 Lincoln Park W, tel. 312/929–5363) for nostalgia's sake. (It had one of the first salad bars.) Others go for the burgers.

2200 N. Cannon Dr., at Lake Shore Dr. and Fullerton Pkwy.

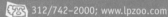 Free

312/742-2000; www.lpzoo.com

Late May–Labor Day, M–F 10–5, Sa–Su 10–6:30; early Sept–late May, daily 10–5

All ages

created and the Great Ape House is being renovated. When the animals return, they'll find natural habitats like the ones their wild relatives call home.

Discovery Stations let children get to know animals by touching related objects, such as a tortoise shell or porcupine quills. For up-close animal encounters, stop at the Children's Zoo, where kids can see newborn animals and those over 5 can even touch some creatures, such as snakes (nonpoisonous ones, of course), a tortoise, and guinea pigs. The Farm-in-the-Zoo could merit its own trip. Here children see firsthand where tomorrow's food comes from—piglets, chicks, and dairy cows. Annual events include Run for the Zoo and ZooFest (June), Spooky Zoo Spectacular (Halloween), and ZooLights Festival and Caroling to the Animals (Christmas). With all of this, it's easy to have a wild time with the animals.

HEY, KIDS! Take a ride on a carousel that has 48 hand-carved animals depicting endangered species, including gorillas and Siberian tigers.

GETTING THERE Free parking is theoretically available but can be hard to find, so you might opt for the paid parking on Cannon Drive. Public transportation is another solution. The No. 151 Sheridan Road bus stops at the zoo. On weekends 9–7, a free trolley runs around the periphery of the zoo and to and from the Fullerton and Sedgewick L stops.

MEXICAN FINE ARTS CENTER MUSEUM

There are no borders at this museum. Everyone is welcome to celebrate Mexican culture, both traditional and contemporary, created in Mexico and in the United States.

The new core of this museum is the permanent exhibit Mexicanidad: Our Past is Present, which displays artifacts, dioramas, and artwork depicting varied aspects of Mexican history—from the indigenous people of the Aztec Empire to Mexican immigrants in the United States. (Mexicanidad refers to the aesthetics, beliefs, and customs that characterize the culture of Mexicans, whether they live in Mexico or elsewhere.) Kids might be frightened by the devil statue in black velvet with sequins, awed by the resplendent gold Spanish colonial altar, and impressed by a 1950s pickup with video of farm-worker activist Cesar Chavez. A multiscreen video at the end traces the significant role of murals in Mexican history. To celebrate Mexicanidad firsthand, head to the Interactive Resource Center, where touch-screen computers let kids see and hear indigenous musical instruments and create their own Día de Muertos (Day of the Dead) altar and sugar skulls.

HEY, KIDS!

Don't be afraid of the special Day of the Dead skulls made of sugar. Mexican kids love them and exchange them with friends like valentines. As part of the event, a Mexican artist demonstrates skull decorating. And since they're made of sugar, they're edible. Yum!

KEEP IN MIND The museum is in the Pilsen neighborhood, which has a large Mexican population. Walking around the area and looking at the stores and restaurants immerses you even further in Mexican culture. Many walls are painted with murals, which as you'll learn from the Mexicanidad exhibit, are messages in the public's face about political and social issues and the celebration of Mexican culture.

 1852 W. 19th St.

 Free

 T–Su 10–5

312/738–1503;
www.mfacmchicago.org

 4 and up

In addition, several other eclectic exhibits grace the museum each year, displaying important archeological finds, folk art, and works by well-known artists. Many of the museum's exhibits are accompanied by free Family Days (some Sundays), which include demonstrations, workshops, and even storytelling sessions for children. In September 2002 the museum will dedicate an outdoor plaza like ones in Mexico to commemorate Mexican-American veterans.

Three times a year, the museum hosts free special events. A Día de Muertos exhibition, late September–early December, displays art inspired by this day when the spirits of those who have died are allowed to return home. An October–November event celebrates the life of Sor Juana, who became an accomplished writer, philosopher, and mathematician in 17th-century Mexico and who has been called the first feminist of the Americas. Activities for children, such as an all-female mariachi-group performance, are usually part of the event. Del Corazon, which means "from the heart," takes place in April and May and includes performing arts events for all ages.

EATS FOR KIDS Mexican restaurants abound. **Nuevo León** (1515 W. 18th St., 312/421– 1517), painted outside with trellises and flowers, serves tacos, enchiladas, tamales, soups, and stews. At **Polo's** (1454 W. 18th St., tel. 312/829–9377), the menu changes daily but always includes traditional Mexican dishes such as chicken with mole sauce and freshly made tortillas. Mexican bakeries make cookies and pastries, and street vendors sell food ranging from warm corn on the cob with lime juice to mango slices.

MILLENNIUM PARK

With the arrival of the new millennium, Chicago's front yard has grown bigger. Though Grant Park was created along the city's lakefront in the 1920s, a nearby railroad yard remained, like an unattractive stepsister who wasn't invited to the ball. Luckily, a Cinderella story has been written, transforming the area into the 24-acre Millennium Park, where the beauty of nature and art intersect to create a peaceful haven and playground for the public.

It's a work in progress. In 2002, a 78-foot by 200-foot skating rink will allow beginners to don skates, glide, fall, and get up again, while experienced skaters practice spins and jumps. You can take the chill off with a visit to the warming house and some hot chocolate from the restaurant, which will have partial service in 2002. In warm weather, the rink transforms into a tent-covered plaza for activities.

Eventually, you'll see art evocative of the past at the Peristyle, a semicircle of classical columns surrounding a pool, designed by Edward H. Bennett (creator of Grant Park's

HEY, KIDS! Look at the Millennium Mosaic, made up of clay tiles created by more than 5,000 adults and children. The designs on the tiles represent each artist's hopes and dreams for the new millennium. If you made a tile, what would you put on it?

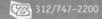
Buckingham Fountain), as well as contemporary art in the form of Anish Kapoor's abstract sculpture. Some people think the 60-foot by 30-foot seamless piece of polished stainless steel looks like a huge jelly bean. You can see the city's skyline and maybe yourself reflected in it; it's rumored to make people look thinner.

You'll also be able to sit on the lawn and enjoy free concerts in a Frank Gehry–designed open-air pavilion, with stainless steel sheets that curl like a gigantic flower in bloom. You can stroll through the Shoulder Garden (think "City of the Big Shoulders"), where a shaded area reflects the city's marshland past and a sunlit one represents its skyscraper present and future. The garden's shape resembles a torso in a suit of armor, with Gehry's bandshell as its fanciful helmet. Kids might see the garden as a whimsical maze of plants that attract birds and butterflies and should love peering out of "windows" in the hedges to see city buildings sprouting before them.

EATS FOR KIDS
A 300-seat **restaurant** is planned for the park. It will begin with a walk-up window to buy sandwiches and snacks, which will open in 2002. For other choices in the area, see the Art Institute of Chicago and the Chicago Cultural Center.

KEEP IN MIND Development of the various aspects of the park is a slow process, with each project finished one by one. So don't expect everything mentioned above to be ready and waiting when you go. The park will have a place to store bikes and an underground parking garage for 2,400 cars.

MITCHELL MUSEUM OF THE AMERICAN INDIAN

The Hollywood stereotypes that once defined Indians are gone, replaced at this museum, part of Kendall College, with a picture of a rich and diverse Native American culture and history. Your children will get a close-up view of native peoples and an understanding of how they used natural resources without exhausting them. Brick walls and red-tile floors give an earthy, you-are-there feeling to the galleries, divided by geographical region.

The French explorers called the Great Lakes tribes the "People of the Rapids" because of their fearless canoeing. The exhibit shows a birch-bark canoe, snowshoes with caribou-hide webbing, and bags decorated with the glass beads that Europeans brought. A table full of "touchables" includes a leather ball that when tossed through a hoop attached to it improves hand-eye coordination—better than video games. Without a Home Depot, Native Americans made their tools, and your kids can try chipping away to sharpen a stone or wearing an anklet of deer toes to attract deer.

KEEP IN MIND Items in the touchable areas are labeled with names and descriptions, but not all the objects are self-explanatory. Ask a museum staff person to explain them.

HEY, KIDS! Try grinding dried corn kernels using a stone, as Native Americans did to make flat bread. It was one of the major occupations of women; in fact, they spent about two hours a day at it. Native Americans have been grinding corn ever since corn came from South America 1,500–2,000 years ago, and some traditionalists still do it today. It's a lot more work to make food this way than to microwave a bag of popcorn, don't you think?

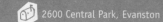 2600 Central Park, Evanston

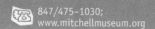 847/475-1030;
www.mitchellmuseum.org

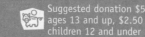 Suggested donation $5
ages 13 and up, $2.50
children 12 and under

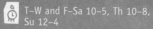 T–W and F–Sa 10–5, Th 10–8,
Su 12–4

 3 and up

Kachina dolls inhabit the Greater Southwest display. The Hopis believed the dolls embodied the spirits of nature and of their ancestors. Among the touchable objects here, the bull roarer is the most impressive. Swinging this piece of wood on a long string makes a truly frightening sound meant to scare wolves.

The tribes of the Plains are represented by elk-skin pants, a feather headdress, and an enormous bison hide. Kids can touch dried antelope hide and see how it was made into moccasins or an arrowhead bag. The Native Americans of the Northwest Coast are represented by monsterlike masks, an authentic totem pole, and a totem-pole puzzle. Children can try on a button blanket, decorated with 450 buttons and worn like a shawl, and can make such crafts as beadwork, soap carving, and sand painting. Special events, including storytelling, music performances, and book discussions, reveal the nuances of Native Americans' culture and close connection to nature.

EATS FOR KIDS Try **Daruma** (2901 Central St., tel. 847/864–6633) for Japanese food, or buy sandwiches from **Foodstuffs** (2106 Central St., tel. 847/328–7704) and eat in the park. **Gino's East** (2516 Green Bay Rd., tel. 847/352–2100) serves up deep-dish pizzas, and **Prairie Joe's** (1921 Central St., tel. 847/491–0391) has kids' fare and unusual stuff on the ceiling.

MUSEUM OF BROADCAST
COMMUNICATIONS

Most kids don't realize that before there was color and cable, there was black and white and rabbit ears, and before that there was radio. Your children can return to those golden olden days, well before they (and you) were born, when families listened not just to music and news but also to dramas and comedy shows. And they listened together.

Start by looking at the old-fashioned radios. Then check out the hands-on displays that make old radio shows accessible to kids. They'll see the ventriloquist dummies Mortimer Snerd and Charlie McCarthy, Jack Benny's sidekicks, and can try to open the safe where the tightwad comedian stashed his cash. But beware. An alarm goes off if they succeed. Open a closet door, and they'll discover what happened when Fibber, in spite of all warnings, opened it each week on "Fibber McGee and Molly" and its contents came tumbling out.

TV has a place here, too. One exhibit showcases puppets from "Garfield Goose and Friends" and other '50s and '60s kids' TV programs as well as the buckets from "Bozo the Clown's

EATS FOR KIDS The building housing the museum has a **Corner Bakery** (*see* the Chicago Cultural Center). The **Big Downtown** (124 S. Wabash Ave., tel. 312/917–7399) has pizzas, sandwiches, hamburgers, and a dessert called the Big Shoulders brownie, named after Carl Sandburg's description of Chicago. Attention-getting city memorabilia enlivens the decor.

Grand Prize Game." Another exhibit covers award-winning commercials. Though they may not convince you to buy the product, they're good for a laugh.

Older children can become news anchors in a TV studio. For $20 each, including a video of the program to take home, your kids can don a sport jacket and read a script on a TelePrompTer in front of a camera. At the end, the child's name appears in the credits. (Call for reservations for any day but Sunday.) At the exhibit celebrating Jack Brickhouse, a legendary Chicago sports announcer known for saying "Hey! Hey!," your children can watch a game on a video screen and record their own play-by-play to take home for a small fee. If you're nostalgic for the old Comiskey Park (replaced in 1990), sit in one of its green seats while you watch a sports program from yesteryear. And for a $3 fee, you and your family can rent a booth and watch old TV programs from the museum's archives. It can be worth it just to all watch TV together.

HEY, KIDS! Once you've seen Bozo, you might just want to clown around a little yourself. The museum store sells big red noses like the one the big goofy clown wore. Ask your parents if they had one when they were little, or even a Bozo punching bag.

KEEP IN MIND Your children might need help relating to the exhibits dealing with the history of radio and TV. If your knowledge doesn't go back further than dials and test patterns, you might want to bring along a grandparent or other older friend, who can share firsthand experiences of the early days of broadcasting.

MUSEUM OF CONTEMPORARY ART

The exterior of this museum isn't very inviting, but once your children get a look at the artworks inside, dating from 1945 to the present, they're sure to think that contemporary art is cool. Some 100 works of the 3,500-piece permanent collection are usually on display. Kids are mesmerized by Alexander Calder's colorful sculptures, intrigued by bizarre surrealist works, and amazed to see vacuum cleaners turned into art. They'll be tempted to plop down on the giant fried-egg soft sculpture, but tell them not to.

Children also discover works where art and technology intersect. They can watch truisms file by on a neon sign and will probably get the giggles watching a video of a woman sucking her toe. A film of a woman's talking head projected onto a ball sticking out from under a mattress on the floor can be disturbing, but then contemporary art can be both humorous and unsettling. To learn more about it, kids can use touch-screen computers to assemble a work of art and play the role of a curator laying out an exhibit.

HEY, KIDS!
Look in the first-floor pond for some beautiful, bright-color Japanese koi fish, which are about a foot long. Why do you think the pond is shaped like an oak leaf? Look up at the shape of the spiral staircase and the skylight and you'll find out.

KEEP IN MIND Not all temporary exhibits are appropriate for children, so call in advance to find out. In addition, some works in the permanent collection contain nudity, deal with adult subject matter, or contain language that you might consider a no-no for your kids. Although the museum does post signs about exhibits that might not be for all viewers, it's not always easy to avoid them. You might want to discuss this possibility with your children beforehand. After all, the goal of some contemporary artists is to be provocative, so use this as an opportunity for conversation.

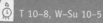 220 E. Chicago Ave.

 $8 adults, $5 students
13 and up; T free

 T 10–8, W–Su 10–5

312/280–2660;
www.mcachicago.org

6 and up

Watch for temporary exhibits, which have featured cartoonlike images, large-scale color transparencies of people on Chicago streets, and photographic sculptures. Exhibits are usually accompanied by free gallery guides, guided tours, and films about the artists, which, though not geared to children, can be enlightening. Pressing buttons on an audio wand ($1 rental) reveals information about various artworks. It's a magical way to decipher the language of contemporary art.

Classes for kids include creating puppets, cartoons, collages, or Web sites. Free Family Sunday Workshops (fall–spring) are inspired by exhibitions or perhaps holidays. Other items of interest include a Family Halloween Benefit, a summer arts camp, and a 24-hour Summer Solstice Festival that features daytime performances for children, chalk-drawing on the plaza, and hands-on creation stations, where kids can make masks and costumes to wear in an extravagant parade led by the life-size puppets and stilt-walkers of Redmoon Theater. Who said art museums were boring?

EATS FOR KIDS The MCA's restaurant is called **Puck's** (tel. 312/397-4034), in honor of Wolfgang Puck, who created the menu. Seasonal items include classics from one of his other restaurants (Spago) and dishes inspired by works at the museum. Kids might enjoy looking for the restaurant's whimsical art before or after they chow down on pizza, sandwiches, and yummy desserts. An Express area has ready-made items. You can eat on the terrace overlooking the sculpture garden.

MUSEUM OF HOLOGRAPHY

Laser technology and art intersect at holography, a relatively new technique whose advancement is the focus of this museum, founded in 1976. Housed in a building west of the Loop, in what used to be an out-of-the-way area and is now becoming gentrified, the museum has a collection of holograms, the equipment for making them, and a school of holography. It's perhaps the only museum of its kind in the country, or maybe the world.

Most kids have seen holograms, those 3-D images on credit cards and stickers, many of which seem to shift when you look at them from different angles. These images are created when light waves are reflected from an object illuminated by the light from lasers and recorded on a light-sensitive medium. This complex technique was discovered accidentally in 1948, but it wasn't until the advent of the laser in the '60s that it gained momentum.

The museum has three exhibition spaces, and exhibits change about once a year. Dimly lit for better viewing, galleries usually include works from the permanent collection. One awe-

EATS FOR KIDS Once a no-man's-land, this gentrifying neighborhood has attracted trendy restaurants for adults. **Wishbone** (1001 W. Washington Blvd., tel. 312/850–2663) can be recognized by big painted panels of a corncob, pig, and turkey. Its "southern reconstruction" cuisine ranges from corn cakes and blackened catfish to fresh-squeezed orange and carrot juices, and there is outdoor seating. **Ina's** (1235 W. Randolph St., tel. 312/226–3304) serves breakfast and soups, salads, and sandwiches for lunch.

1134 W. Washington Blvd.

 $3.50 adults 19 and up,
$2.50 children 6–18

312/226–1007;
www.holographiccenter.com

 W–Su 12:30–4:30

6 and up

inspiring example is a large image of a man bending down to pan for gold. As you walk past it, the gold miner moves his hand, scoops up some water, and looks to see if he has any gold nuggets. The hologram contains about 300 movements in all. Walk back and forth several times to fully appreciate it.

Another impressive hologram is a gigantic *Tyrannosaurus rex* skull with a mouth full of enormous teeth. Because he looks as though he's looming, ready to take a bite, he might frighten some kids. Still other holograms are in transparent cylinders. In one, Michael Jordan seems to turn around and pass a basketball behind his back.

The old saying has it that seeing is believing, and you'll be sorely tempted to believe that many of these holographic images are "real." They're not, of course, and it makes the experience of viewing them downright eerie.

HEY, KIDS! You'll probably be very tempted to touch the holograms to see if they're "real." But please don't. Fingerprints are a problem on the glass protecting them. And besides, it's against the rules. If you're interested in holography as a career, when you're done with high school, you can attend the museum's school. It takes three 10-week semesters to fully learn how to make holograms, which are used not only by artists, but also in medicine, engineering, architecture, and advertising.

KEEP IN MIND
To help children see holograms best, have them take their time and stand about 5 feet away. The museum isn't usually crowded, so this shouldn't be a problem. To see holograms shift or transform, kids should move slowly from side to side or back and forth.

MUSEUM OF SCIENCE AND INDUSTRY

I mpressive kid-friendly technology starts in the parking garage, home to the *Pioneer Zephyr*. In 1934, this streamlined train, nicknamed the "Silver Streak," made a nonstop run from Denver to Chicago in a record-breaking 13 hours, 4 minutes, and 56 seconds. Your children can hop aboard this first diesel-electric train and feel its rocking motion and then go into the engineer's cab and pretend to be in control. From here it's up the escalator to see a more contemporary form of travel: a replica of the 22-foot-tall Cassini Space Probe, launched in 1997 and scheduled to orbit Saturn in 2004.

But that's just the beginning. At the Coal Mine, an elevator ride simulates a trip deep into the earth, and it's dark down there. At the bottom, a small train like those that miners rode takes you to see what mining was like in the 1930s. Another exhibit takes you "underwater" in a German U-505 submarine from World War II. In Time, timepieces range from sundials to jeweled watches to the atomic clock, and the twelve disciples emerge from a 19th-century German clock at noon. In Networld, kids put their own face on a

EATS FOR KIDS Museum eateries include a **Pizza Hut;** an authentic 1917 **ice-cream parlor,** inside the Yesterday's Main Street exhibit; and the **Astro Cafe.** Near the Omnimax theater, it carries hot dogs, hamburgers, pizzas, and nachos. An outdoor patio is open in good weather.

KEEP IN MIND The museum is big, so take breaks to rest, eat, and see an Omnimax movie. (For the same price as the movie, you can opt for an evening Omnilaser Fantasy light show featuring rock music.) To ensure tickets, reserve in advance. Even ticket holders begin lining up 15–20 minutes early. Many people think the best seats are high up and in the middle. Speaking of tickets, so that the Idea Factory doesn't get too crowded, free, timed tickets are available at the exhibit entrance, and there are rest rooms and a nursing room within the exhibit, so you won't have to leave before you're ready.

cartoon character and follow the figure through the inner workings of computers and the Internet. In Genetics: Decoding Life, children see genetically engineered animals and can ponder how science will shape our future.

Though most everything in the museum appeals to children, there's also a special area, the Idea Factory, especially for them. If you have an infant, head for an enclosed space with toys where even the smallest scientist can discover the wonders of the world. Children 10 and under can explore light, color, and especially water in an area with a stream that's perfect for floating boats they build or manipulating pumps and wheels, locks and dams. The pièce de résistance is an enormous contraption with levers, cranks, gears, and buttons that produce amazing effects. No visit to the museum is complete, however, without being enveloped by an Omnimax film depicting the natural wonders of the earth, sky, and sea. It puts science and industry into stunning perspective.

HEY, KIDS! There are a lot of big, spectacular things to see at the museum, but take time for little things, too. One such is the Fairy Castle, which was donated to the museum in 1949 by Hollywood movie star Colleen Moore. Its seven rooms, which have electricity and running water no less, are decorated with tiny treasures. Enjoy the fun of the animals and acrobats in a small animated circus, too.

Navy Pier was built in 1916 for commercial ships, but after years of standing unused, it was transformed in 1995 into a place to have fun. Though people do come in winter, summer sees the biggest festivities and the biggest crowds. In fact, it can be a challenge just to stroll the walkways (be sure to keep your children close), but the hustle and bustle can be part of the pleasure.

Vendors sell snack food, and kids can make crafts like masks, hats, and baseball banners for free—daily in summer and on weekends in winter. Wherever you go you'll run into free entertainment by jugglers, magicians, clowns, and groups such as the the Dock Street Stompers and an improv group called A Piering Daily. There is never a dull moment. A miniature golf course has 18 holes, Amazing Chicago lets you wander through a maze of city landmarks complete with special effects, the Time Escape ride takes a trip through Chicago's past, the carousel has so many unusual hand-painted animals that kids find it hard to choose, and the slow-moving Ferris wheel lets everyone appreciate the view. Cap off your day with

EATS FOR KIDS Along with other pier eateries (*see* Chicago Children's Museum), **Bubba Gump Shrimp Co.** (tel. 312/595–5500), inspired by the movie *Forrest Gump*, offers shrimp, burgers, and a box of chocolates. Show the side of the license plate you're given that says "Stop, Forrest, Stop" if you need service, "Run, Forrest, Run" if you're fine. Children work at place mats with Gump-y games or look at movie memorabilia or the film itself, which plays continuously with the sound down. As you leave, take a picture on the bench with Forrest's suitcase and chocolate box.

fireworks, given Wednesdays and Saturdays in summer. Make a special trip for family activities celebrating Halloween, the winter holidays, New Year's Eve and Day, and Kid's Day, in February.

The pier is also home to the Chicago Children's Museum (*see* #60) and to the Cineplex Odeon's IMAX Theater (tel. 312/444–FILM), which shows not only traditional IMAX films on its six-story, 80-foot-wide screen, but also 3-D movies.

Inside the pier building, take a peek at the free Museum of Stained Glass Windows, where beautiful multicolor windows recovered from buildings that were being torn down paint a picture of Chicago history. Shops galore include the Chicago Children's Museum store, a magic shop, a place that sells crazy hats, and another that does hair wraps and sells glittery nail polish. And in case you think there's nothing new under the sun in winter, come skate on the open-air ice rink.

HEY, KIDS! Walk all the way to the end of the pier, and look around you. Do you feel like you're standing in the middle of Lake Michigan? That's not surprising. You've come 3,000 feet out from the shore.

GETTING THERE Parking at Navy Pier is limited and expensive ($7.50 for the first hour). Try to find parking in lots or on the streets west of the museum. It may be several long blocks away, so take the free trolley that runs west on Grand Avenue to State Street and then back east on Illinois Street. Another option is to take a CTA bus here: No. 29 State Street, No. 56 Milwaukee Avenue, No. 65 Grand Avenue, No. 66 Chicago Avenue, No. 120 Northwestern Train Station, and No. 121 Union Station.

NEW MAXWELL STREET MARKET

If your children are old enough to appreciate browsing as opposed to buying and won't subject you to an endless stream of "Can I have . . . ," then a Sunday spent at this open-air market can be a great family outing. The first Maxwell Street Market developed in a Jewish neighborhood in the early 1900s. Vendors pushed carts full of merchandise and sold fruits and vegetables from stands in the streets. Though the first location was gobbled up by urban development, a new market grew up nearby in 1994. It is as much a piece of urban folklore as it is a place of commerce, and people come to rummage through new and used stuff alike in search of bargains and hidden antiques.

The market is a microcosm of Chicago, a concept that will probably be lost on children younger than observant teens. Recent and not-so-recent immigrants—plenty of Spanish-speaking people, some Asians, and African-Americans—try to catch hold of the American

EATS FOR KIDS Not surprisingly, the food sold at stands here is eclectic. There are hot dogs and Polish sausages, steak burgers, tacos, and egg rolls. In warm weather, you can get ice cream.

GETTING THERE If you buy bulky items, you'll need a car, but as always, driving and parking aren't easy. Canal Street around the market is closed, but side streets are manageable. Parking options include lots on 14th Place between Clinton and Canal streets and at the River West Plaza at Roosevelt Road and Jefferson Street, metered parking on Roosevelt between Clinton and Des Plaines, and free diagonal parking on Clinton between Taylor and Roosevelt. Free diagonal parking is also available April–October on Clinton between Polk and Taylor and on Des Plaines from Taylor to Roosevelt.

 Canal St. between Taylor St. and Depot Pl.

 Free

 Su 7–3

312/922–3100 for map;
www.cityofchicago.org/consumerservices

6 and up

dream or just earn some ready cash. Senior citizens try to scrounge for a few extra dollars. Your children can uncover brand-new toys and ones that have been slightly abused, new and used video games, stuffed animals, and used bikes. There are small trinkets like key chains with cartoon characters and refrigerator magnets that play jingles. There are clothes and shoes for all ages, as well as such necessities as toilets and car tires. The pleasure is in the search.

Musicians perform and pass the hat, and chances are good that you'll hear some blues— a staple of the market for years—along with Peruvian flute and perhaps some alternative rock. A sketch artist sometimes sets up an easel. But kids just like to soak up the activity and maybe dream of finding that special treasure.

KEEP IN MIND There is a lot of hustle and bustle here. In fact, approximately 20,000 people come to the market every Sunday, so warn your kids to stay close so as not to get lost. Advise them that if you become separated, they should seek out one of the market's zone managers, who wear a New Maxwell Street Market badge on their shirts or jackets, or a security officer with a badge. Set up a clear meeting spot and time with older kids who are allowed to go off on their own; it gets far too crowded to count on running into each other.

NORTH AVENUE BEACH

19

Chicago has a glorious natural resource: 20 miles of Lake Michigan shoreline dotted with 30 sandy beaches. The beaches differ, ranging from Calumet Beach, at the city's southern tip, which has a vista of factories and smokestacks, to the small Oak Street Beach, at Oak Street and Lake Shore Drive, where fit 20- and 30-somethings show off their sleek, tan bodies, to a smattering of mini beaches at the end of residential streets to the north. (Beaches in the suburbs along the North Shore charge admission.) North Avenue Beach, on the other hand, attracts mostly families—so many, in fact, that it's a good idea to come early to get a parking space and stake out a place on the beach.

This wide expanse of clean, soft, fine sand, nearly a mile long, has a backdrop of beautiful high-rises, vintage buildings, and the natural landscape of Lincoln Park. The water is shallow near the shore, so timid tots can safely dip their toes. Even farther out, the lake bottom is still sandy, so there's no stumbling on pebbles and stones. While young professionals play volleyball and work out at an open-air fitness center, kids play endlessly in the sand and water.

EATS FOR KIDS The **Castaways Cafe** (tel. 773/281–1200), on the rooftop of the beach house, has a spectacular view. Kids can find hamburgers and chicken wings; adults might prefer the Jamaican jerk chicken or salads. It's a good place for refreshing ice cream, too. Concession stands sell snacks and soft drinks. If you're ready to move on, the nearby Lincoln Park Zoo (*see #29*) has a number of places to eat.

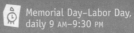

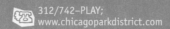

The beach is easy to spot from a distance. Just look for the beach house shaped like an old-fashioned ocean liner, complete with blue portholes and red smokestacks. In addition to inspiring the imagination, the facility contains the basic necessities: rest rooms and snack bars.

The water is cold at the beginning of summer but warms up gradually as the season progresses. In mid-August, crowds arrive for the Air and Water Show. Throngs of thrill-seekers come to crane their necks and watch precision flying teams and old-time and high-tech planes. The noise can be deafening. So if you'd rather have your sun and sand without the show, come at another time. There's no better place than this beach on a hot summer day.

HEY, KIDS! See that building sticking out of the water way out in the lake? It's not a home for mermaids or sea monsters. It's a pumping station that takes lake water and sends it to a filtration plant, where it's cleaned so it's safe enough to drink.

KEEP IN MIND Even though lifeguards are on duty, you should keep a close eye on your children. The lake is full of ever-changing surprises. Sometimes you'll find choppy waves or an undertow. The bottom shifts, too, so where you once found a gradual deepening might now be a steep drop-off that can catch everyone, especially children, off guard.

NORTH BRANCH BICYCLE TRAIL

18

This 20-mile Cook County Forest Preserve Trail stretches from Chicago all the way north to Lake County through a variety of landscapes. The paved trail, made especially for families, is flat or gently sloping—no Tour de France, here.

The trail traverses Caldwell Woods along the North Branch of the Chicago River. Just north of Devon Avenue at the beginning of the trail, a flat-woods area contains old pin oaks and swamp white oaks as well as spring flowers such as trillium, trout lily, and wild geranium. The area between Devon and Touhy avenues is a savanna, common in Illinois 200 years ago.

The trail continues past the summertime swimmers at Whealan Aquatic Center (one place where trail access is near parking) and on through Miami Woods in Skokie and Linne Woods in Morton Grove. The trail through Miami Woods, north of Oakton Street, passes by the eastern edge of an approximately 20-acre natural prairie—a slice of Illinois as it was before settlers arrived. Grasses grow, and in August the flowering stalks are over 6 feet tall.

EATS FOR KIDS To make your outing complete, take along a picnic lunch. If you'd prefer, though, you can ride to the Chicago Botanic Garden, which has a café with outdoor seating.

KEEP IN MIND Call ahead to get a trail map. Then read the rules for biking and explain them to your children. Stay to the right, and ride single file, warning others before you pass. Obey all stop signs. The speed limit is 8 mph, and no racing is allowed. Children should not disturb the native landscape. Flowers should not be picked, and fallen trees should be left where they are, to make good homes and food for wildlife and nourish the soil, too. If you go for a walk, stay on the paths, or you may encounter poison ivy.

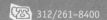

Next comes the Chick Evans Golf Course and Harms Woods, just north of Golf Road, where you might see horseback riders on their own trail, parallel to the bike path. Stables are nearby. Continue on to Glenview and Blue Star Memorial woods before arriving at the Skokie Lagoons, created by the Civilian Conservation Corps during the Depression. The lagoons, where people go canoeing and rowing, are home to sandpipers, egrets, and heron. Farther north, the trail ends at the formal Chicago Botanic Garden (*see* #61).

If you've gotten the idea that the trail threads through pure nature, without housing developments and office buildings, you're right. All along it are places to picnic, rest, and drink well water. Pick a section of path or ride it all if you want to, but bike it again at different times of year to see the landscape change.

HEY, KIDS! Though the trail is home to possums, raccoons, beaver, mink, muskrats, and owls, you won't see them by day. More likely are rabbits, gray and fox squirrels, and chipmunks. Deer here are fearless. Since much of their natural habitat has been developed, the areas along the bike trail have become their home and their pathway along the river. You might also hear warblers. If you stop and walk to the river, you can see ducks, various turtles, green frogs, and bullfrogs.

NORTH PARK VILLAGE NATURE CENTER

This nature preserve is a haven, both for wildlife and the humans who come here to take a break from civilization. Four ecosystems are contained within it—wetland, oak savanna, prairie, and woodland—and the vegetation you and your children will find as you walk from one ecosystem to another varies widely.

More than 7,000 native plants grow in front of the nature center in gardens that represent a microcosm of the preserve's ecosystems, but there are also three other gardens. In one, plants such as wild bergamot and prairie blazing star have been chosen because they attract black swallowtails, monarchs, and other butterflies. A Native American garden, with a wigwam nearby, has pale purple coneflower and goldenseal, which Native Americans used in medicines. A vegetable garden features plants you can grow in your own backyard.

The preserve is also home to toads, turtles, salamanders, rabbits, deer, and lots of birds, so your kids should keep an eye peeled. If you come at the right time, you can get help

KEEP IN MIND After you've seen the gardens here, think about whether you'd like to add any of these plants to your backyard. Native plants are good choices, because they're so well adapted to this climate. Flowers and other plants that attract birds and butterflies can produce fascinating activity along with color. Besides, it's fun to garden with more than "looks" in mind.

from the nature center staff and performers, who regularly offer such family events as spider walks, turtle programs, and campfire storytelling and sing-alongs. Free seasonal events, such as those honoring maple sugaring, Earth Month, the fall harvest, and the winter solstice, include crafts, games, and storytelling. Many activities are based on Native American culture.

If your children didn't see enough on the trails or want to get a preview of coming attractions before your walk, venture inside the nature center, where you can get a close-up look at some of the types of small animals that live in the surrounding environment. Indoor and outdoor beehives show how bees live and why they make honey. An outdoor bird aviary contains some examples of the feathered friends that live in the preserve or that stop by on their way north or south. The nature center is a nice place for your family to stop by, too.

EATS FOR KIDS
Though the center sells no food, it has several picnic tables and a grassy space in the shade of an oak tree. For a fast bite nearby, head to **McDonald's** (3241 W. Peterson Ave., tel. 773/588–8860) or **Arby's** (2938 W. Peterson Ave., tel. 773/761–9438).

HEY, KIDS! Pay your respects to the center's green heron, who lives in a cage outdoors in summer and indoors when the weather gets cold. He was brought here 20 years ago with an injured wing and has stayed because he couldn't survive in the wild. Though his long beak is made for fishing, he doesn't have to do his own anymore. Staff members feed him live fish each morning. You might spy a heron in one of the preserve's ponds.

ORIENTAL INSTITUTE MUSEUM

This museum is housed in a three-story neo-Gothic building similar to the other buildings on the University of Chicago campus. Its five galleries devoted to ancient civilizations were closed in 1996 for renovation.

The first gallery to reopen (in 1998) was the Egyptian Gallery, where a colossal 17-foot statue of King Tut towers. Children can walk around him, noticing the things he wears that are different from what men wear today: a pleated skirt, a dagger with a falcon head, a striped head cloth, and a cobra rearing up on his forehead, supposedly for protection. Other objects reveal similarities between the ancient Egyptians and us. There are statues of a police chief and several bakers as well as jewelry that most women would be happy to wear today, except perhaps for the extra-large earrings. There is also a tunic and a pair of shoes worn by an Egyptian child long ago. Egyptian games include one carved like a coiled snake. Adult mummies are here, but so is an intricately wrapped one of a child, demonstrating how much children were valued in ancient Egypt. Have your kids look for the mummy

KEEP IN MIND Large information sheets, available near each major object, feature full-color reproductions of the object, point out special features your kids can look for, and pose thought-provoking questions that will get them to think like an archaeologist.

HEY, KIDS! The museum has computers with games, puzzles, and other activities about objects from Persia and Egypt. You can find out what the symbols on the mummy cases (called sarcophagi) mean and even decorate a mummy case yourself. You can also look inside one of the mummies, thanks to a computer program that shows you the results of a CAT scan and X ray. If you want to continue your exploration, you can e-mail information to yourself at home, where you can read more about what interests you and save materials for homework projects.

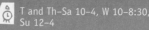

of a crocodile. It's partially unwrapped so the head is visible. Child-friendly descriptions, self-guided tours, and treasure hunts help kids focus on the details.

A gallery of artifacts from ancient Persia (modern-day Iran) is also now open. These include a series of gigantic polished black limestone sculptures, including the head of a bull that guarded the entrance to the Hundred-Column Hall. Artifacts from ancient Mesopotamia (today's Iraq), including a 40-ton (yes, 40-ton) bull and wall sculptures depicting the king, his servants, and soldiers, are expected by summer 2002. Exhibits documenting the ancient civilizations of Nubia, Turkey, and Israel should be open by 2003.

Family days occur four times a year. One in summer is held in conjunction with the Smart Museum, which houses Asian and European art, and Halloween brings the Mummies Night. Hands-on workshops, performances, and films are also offered.

EATS FOR KIDS The **Reynolds Club** (5706 S. University Ave., tel. 773/702–8787), also in a neo-Gothic campus building, has a food court with pizza, tacos, and Chinese food. A wood-paneled dining room has portraits of university presidents. The **Nile Restaurant** (1611 E. 55th St., tel. 773/324–9499) roams beyond Egypt. Middle Eastern dishes include hummus, stuffed grape leaves, tabbouleh, and shish kebabs. Children like the *shawerma* (marinated, rotisserie-cooked, shredded chicken).

PEACE MUSEUM

At a time when TV, movies, and video games make violence seem normal, when bullies and their victims make headlines, and when youngsters use guns to solve problems, the Peace Museum offers another perspective. It was founded in 1981 by Mark Rogovin, a Chicago muralist, and Marjorie Craig Benton, then U.S. ambassador to the United Nations International Emergency Fund. Their mission was to show the horrors of nuclear war and other life-destroying forces, ways that activists and artists worldwide work for peace, and how all people can learn to live peacefully.

In spring 2001 the Peace Museum spread its wings and moved out of its cramped original home on the Near North Side, becoming an Arts Partner with the Chicago Park District, which provided office and storage space and the opportunity to display exhibitions in a number of its field houses. Today you might find exhibits in Garfield Park (100 N. Central Park Ave.), Douglas Park (1401 S. Sacramento Blvd.), or LaFollette Park (1333 N. Laramie Ave.), on the West Side.

KEEP IN MIND Because the Peace Museum offers children role models and information about conflict resolution and creative ways to express their feelings, take this as an opportunity to talk to them about how the exhibits' themes relate to problems in their own lives. Do some brainstorming to find peaceful ways of solving them. Some exhibits, such as those displaying the destruction left by atomic bombs, can be troubling, so be prepared to discuss how your kids feel about what they saw. You could suggest they create artwork to express their feelings when they get home.

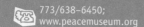 Various Chicago Park District locations

 Free

 M–F 9–9, Sa–Su 9–5

773/638-6450;
www.peacemuseum.org

 8 and up, but varies
by exhibit

Since the museum, perhaps the only one of its kind in the country, has a permanent collection of more than 10,000 artworks, artifacts, and historical items, it has no trouble mounting two or three exhibits at a time, which remain on display for several months. The museum has photographs, posters, and pamphlets depicting the work of civil rights leader Martin Luther King, Jr., and items illustrating the career of acclaimed singer, actor, football player, and activist Paul Robeson. The collection contains drawings by survivors of the Hiroshima and Nagasaki atomic bombs as well as many of the anti–nuclear war panels that were put together to form a ribbon around the Pentagon in 1985. In addition, the collection includes memorabilia from such musicians as John Lennon, who urged listeners to "give peace a chance." Ironically, the Beatle died a violent death in 1980, but his plea is as meaningful as ever today. Indeed the Peace Museum's exhibits will show your kids many ways they can give peace a chance.

HEY, KIDS! Some peacemakers are very well known, but others are just ordinary people whose names aren't ever in the headlines. Do you know any peacemakers at your school or in your neighborhood?

EATS FOR KIDS Exhibitions often take place in the West Side neighborhood, where family-friendly restaurants are scarce. See the Garfield Park Conservatory for ones that are a short car ride away.

Chicago is hiding something, a not-so-secret system of underground walkways that has become almost a city unto itself, containing stores, restaurants, and other places of business. In the early 1950s the city started building tunnels to connect subway stations, and, like a monster, the Pedway just kept growing. It will probably keep expanding beyond its current size, a warren of 23 blocks that children, and adults, like to explore. As many commuters can attest—they use the Pedway to get between trains or subways and their offices without braving the elements—there are many entrances to this maze. A convenient one is at the State Street subway station, between Randolph and Washington streets. To find other entrances, consult the map, available from the information center in the Chicago Cultural Center (*see* #59), which just happens to be above the Pedway. If you're ever lost, simply look for an exit and go up to street level, where you'll soon get your bearings.

Walking along the stretch west of State Street, you'll find a little of everything: a newsstand that sells snacks and fresh fruits; a barber shop; a Starbucks; a blind person selling

KEEP IN MIND Though there are many stores in the Pedway, remind your kids that the most interesting aspect of these underground corridors is that they are like a maze. Encourage them to treat a visit as an enjoyable, challenging game rather than a shopping spree.

EATS FOR KIDS On the Pedway's west side, on the Daley Center lower level, **West Egg Cafe** (66 W. Washington St., tel. 312/236–3322) specializes in omelets for breakfast, but it serves other meals, too. Kids like the gourmet pancakes, including Strawnana Cakes and Berried Treasures. **Houlihan's** (111 E. Wacker Dr., tel. 312/616–FOOD) has a standard kid's menu. Depending on where you are, also check out the eating options under the Art Institute of Chicago, Chicago Cultural Center, Millennium Park, and Sculpture Alfresco Walking Tour.

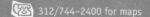

newspapers; a big gift store with stuffed animals, balloons with messages on them, and gourmet suckers in unusual flavors; and a food court with an eclectic selection.

If you go east from State Street, you'll pass by the lower level of Marshall Field's and then on down a hallway with lots of shops. Beneath the Chicago Cultural Center, your children can look through the window of a radio station, where people are broadcasting books for the blind to listen to. They can also see a changing exhibit of artwork by Chicago children, who may have made self-portraits, quilts, or multimedia works inspired by the Chicago River. Farther along, at the Athletic Club, kids can see a seven-story climbing wall; come at lunchtime to see office workers work out.

Like a city, the Pedway seemingly has neighborhoods. The eastern section, which travels under several hotels, is the most elegant and has a shopping concourse. Also like a city, the Pedway is a good place to wander, discovering surprises all along the way.

HEY, KIDS! Here's a fun game: First, make sure your parents get a map of the Pedway. (They'll want one anyway, to navigate the corridors without getting too confused.) Then pause in a spot and try to guess what's above ground there. Try to picture all the people over your head and what they might be doing. Your parents can look at the map and tell you if you're right.

PEGGY NOTEBAERT NATURE MUSEUM

This nature museum, founded in 1857 as the Chicago Academy of Sciences, is the oldest museum in Chicago, but that doesn't mean it's over the hill. In fact, its modern earth-tone building near the Lincoln Park Zoo (*see #29* for parking suggestions) has many new exhibits as well as some old favorites.

As you stroll through the Butterfly Haven, you'll see a United Nations of beautiful creatures: painted ladies and red admirals from the Midwest, blue butterflies with a 6-inch wingspan from Central and South America, and rice paper butterflies from Asia. Youngsters can watch butterflies feed and find chrysalises, caterpillars, and eggs (with a magnifying glass). Nearby, kids can discover monarchs' migration paths and smell the odor that swallowtail caterpillars emit to keep enemies away.

Kids learn more about the Midwest at the Water Lab, featuring a model of a river. They can create acid rain; learn about Lake Michigan's inhabitants, including undesirable zebra mussels

HEY, KIDS! Once you've learned something about nature in the Midwest, go out on one of the museum's terraces and see if you can spot five different ecological communities—prairie, pond, ravine, moist woodland, and dunes—in the surrounding landscape.

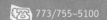 Fullerton Pkwy. and Cannon Dr.

773/755-5100

$6 ages 15 and up, $3 children 3–14 and students

 Th–T 10–5 (Memorial Day–Labor Day, to 6), W 10–8

3 and up

and alewives; and look at drops of water through a microscope. In City Science, your family can find out who else lives in your house with you. You'll learn the difference between good and bad bacteria and see what lurks beneath your basement. The well-liked dioramas are back in an area called the Wilderness Walk, where you travel through Illinois's ecosystems.

Anyone with young children should head to the Children's Gallery. Chances are they'll be overjoyed to put on a beaver costume and find out firsthand about these famed tree gnawers. They can play among the soft-sculpture flowers and tall grasses of a make-believe prairie and search a mural to find well-camouflaged animals. In a setting purported to be under a prairie, they can see the roots of prairie plants overhead and learn about the snakes and ant colonies that dwell underground. And if anyone gets tired, you can rest in comfortable areas nearby and read a book.

EATS FOR KIDS
The museum's **Butterfly Cafe** turns out gourmet sandwiches and salads for grown-ups as well as peanut butter and jelly sandwiches, hot dogs, pasta with red sauce, and other kid-friendly items. For other eating options, *see* the Lincoln Park Zoo.

KEEP IN MIND To give your children the best chance of seeing butterflies up close, remind them to be as quiet and still as possible in the Butterfly Haven. These beauties are skittish and don't tend to stick around when loud and boisterous youngsters are being loud and boisterous.

RAINBOW FALLS WATER PARK

Water, water everywhere, and all of it's for play. This water park and adjacent miniature golf course cover 5½ acres. Your kids won't know where to start splashing and sliding first. They can rush pell-mell down three different flume slides or climb up a platform made of make-believe boulders to dive into an L-shape pool. The Lazy River isn't completely lazy; after swirling along for 300 feet, floaters head down chutes to a splash landing. Water cannons await pretend pirates, and tunnels await those seeking to hide from the scoundrels. Young Tarzans and Janes can swing through the air, landing not in a jungle, but in refreshing water.

The welcome mat's always out at the cheery, three-story, purple, yellow, and turquoise Funhouse. It's just like a carnival fun house, with surprises when you least expect them. Just when kids thought it was safe to get back out of the water, someone might spray them—or perhaps they'll dump a bucketful on someone else. The atmosphere of suspense is heightened by a big bowl on the roof, 32 feet above, which slowly fills with water

KEEP IN MIND Contrary to what you might think, weekdays are the most crowded here, because busloads of campers come to play. Luckily, some Mondays don't have camp groups, and weekends are good for families, too. Waits for activities are usually no more than several minutes.

EATS FOR KIDS The **Splash Cafe** concession stand has quick snacks, such as popcorn and pretzels, and easy-to-eat meals like pizza and nachos. There are tables shaded by umbrellas as well as some grassy areas with picnic tables nearby. If you want a more peaceful time-out, you can take your food and climb aboard the River Queen, a replica of a Mississippi River paddleboat, to eat. If you prefer, instead of buying food at the concession stand, you can bring your own picnic.

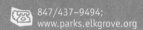
100 Lions Dr., Elk Grove Village

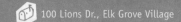
847/437-9494;
www.parks.elkgrove.org

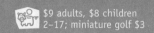
$9 adults, $8 children
2-17; miniature golf $3

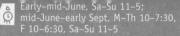
Early-mid-June, Sa-Su 11-5;
mid-June-early Sept, M-Th 10-7:30,
F 10-6:30, Sa-Su 11-5

2 and up

and then every few minutes, tips over, spilling it on everyone below. For more action, a tube ride hurtles kids down 80 feet into a cool pool. Older kids love the Funhouse, but so do some parents, particularly when accompanying adventuresome toddlers who giggle with delight.

Little H_2O lovers, up to age 7, have places that are meant just for them in the Children's Adventure Pool. There's a junior water slide, a spraying turtle that doubles as a slide, tunnels, and a gentle tube ride. Toddlers can experiment with the water experience just a little bit, but not too much, in a wading pool.

When your kids get waterlogged, it's time to dry off for a game of miniature golf. (The park has showers and changing areas.) Perhaps too challenging for kids under 5, the course has some difficult holes, some where the hole itself can't be seen from the tee and one where you have to hit the ball over, what else—water.

HEY, KIDS! Some kids like water a lot and some like it just a little, so only splash (or spray) those who want to be splashed, and be gentle with the others. Don't forget that, for safety's sake, running isn't allowed. You have to know how to swim to go on the water slides and the tube rides. Lifeguards keep watch to make sure the rule is adhered to, but that doesn't mean you can't have fun doing all the other activities.

ROSENBAUM ARTIFACT CENTER

The Spertus Museum, with a permanent collection of approximately 10,000 artworks and artifacts, focuses on the history of Jewish religion and culture spanning the globe and the centuries, from antiquity to contemporary times. Children, Jewish and gentile alike, can learn a lot about Judaism here, seeing beautiful objects whose purposes they may or may not be familiar with. But they can discover even more—and on their own—in the museum's Rosenbaum ARTiFACT Center.

Here kids can dig up artifacts in an archaeological mound, with 12 trenches representing different periods from 1280 to 200 BC. They can use digging tools to search the site's layers and a sieve to sift the sand, revealing old coins, pottery shards, and other relics. Kids can then take their finds to a lab to learn about the clues archaeologists use to identify the age of pottery and can look in drawers representing different time periods to find other objects and information. The result is a picture of how people lived long ago in the area that is now Israel.

HEY, KIDS! We don't have CDs of the songs Jewish people played centuries ago, but we do know what their musical instruments looked like. You can try out reproductions of 22 ancient instruments and press buttons to hear other people playing them. You can also make your own instruments: a drum out of a coffee tin, a rattle from dry macaroni in a paper cup, and a lyre with cardboard and rubber bands. Try making up your own tune, too.

 Spertus Museum, 618 S. Michigan Ave.

$5 adults, $3 students
5 and up

 Su–Th 1–4:30 and some Th evenings;
museum Su–W 10–5, Th 10–8, F 10–3

312/322–1747; www.spertus.edu

3–12

In Family Life at the Oasis, youngsters go back 2,500 years to the time when Israelites, who had been exiled by the Babylonians, returned to their land. Kids open doors in a map to find answers to questions children asked their parents on their journey home. This is the place to discover what Israelites used to heal wounds and what children did when they were bored. If you listen, you'll hear the sounds of birds, the wind, laughter, and a flute.

The Israelite House is designed for preschoolers. Here little ones can look for artifacts in a site meant for little hands, climb onto a make-believe camel, try on clothing, pretend to bake bread in a small oven, and make up stories and perform them with puppets. Special activities, for which there's an additional fee (usually $5), are scheduled regularly and may include making scenes from ancient Israel inside a shoe box, a house sculpture out of clay, or a woven bag. Children become time travelers, and their pretend games re-create bygone eras.

KEEP IN MIND
If your kids are 12 or older, you might want to visit the Zell Holocaust Memorial in the Spertus Museum. It's not designed with children in mind, however, so the artifacts, photos, and video might be too disturbing for sensitive youths. It's best to prepare your kids for the experience beforehand and accompany them throughout.

EATS FOR KIDS The Italian-flavored kids' menu at **Trattoria Caterina** (616 S. Dearborn St., tel. 312/939–7606) includes pizza, pasta with butter, and pasta marinara with a meatball. For a snack of lemon or turtle cookies and juice, try **Gourmand** (728 S. Dearborn St., tel. 312/427–2610). *Also see* Chicago Playworks.

RYERSON WOODS

Ryerson Woods is two things in one. It's both a beautiful natural setting and a farm with domesticated animals. Start by getting a map at the visitor center, a lovely Greek Revival mansion built by the Edward L. Ryerson family, who donated property for part of this conservation area in 1966. (In subsequent years, other families donated land to the Lake County Forest Preserve, which purchased some itself, and 550-acre Ryerson Woods opened in 1972.) With map in hand, start a careful exploration of this environmentally sensitive land.

Junior naturalists will enjoy walking along 6 miles of trails through land that is home to more than 150 kinds of birds and 500 different plants. One trail meanders through a forest and along the banks of the Des Plaines River, so animals can be spotted both on land and over the water. Another trail, which is wheelchair accessible, goes through the prairie and along the edge of the woods. The visitor center provides a tape, which can be used free of charge, that points out interesting details along this trail.

HEY, KIDS!
Take a look in the two log cabins, which have exhibits that change according to the seasons. Here you can touch a beaver skin and the antler of a deer and look closely at an owl prepared by a taxidermist. Pretty neat, huh?

KEEP IN MIND Ryerson Woods is the habitat for many endangered species, including the purple-fringed orchid, dog violets, the red-shouldered hawk, and the Eastern Massasauga rattlesnake. (Never fear, these snakes live far from the trails and avoid contact with humans.) As a result, the familiar motto—Take nothing but pictures, leave nothing but footprints—applies here. Picking and collecting plants is prohibited, as are pets, picnics, fishing, horses, bicycles, and snowmobiles. It's important to stay on the trails to protect the very rare woodland as well as to avoid poison ivy.

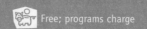
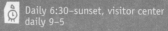
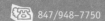

For a different experience, head to Ryerson's barn, where your children can hear the real versions of Old McDonald's farm sounds. The turkey goes "gobble, gobble"; the sheep says "baa, baa"; and some chickens, pigs, cows, and a goat add their own distinctive voices to the chorus.

Depending on the time of year you visit, there will be something different to see and do. The maple forest is splendid in the fall. In early summer, a small piece of prairie is a field of tall grasses, but by late summer its flowers are in full bloom. Cross-country skiers are welcome in the winter whenever there is at least 4 inches of snow. Annual events, ranging from sheep shearing to a Halloween Hike, and less elaborate family programs are held throughout the year. But whenever you visit, Ryerson Woods is a great place to get to know Mother Nature firsthand.

EATS FOR KIDS Picnics aren't allowed at Ryerson Woods. For '50s nostalgia and food, try **Ed Debevic's Short Order Deluxe** (600 Lake Cook Rd., tel. 847/945–3242). **Flatlander's** (Milwaukee Ave. and Old Half Day Rd., Lincolnshire, tel. 847/821–1234), in a setting inspired by Frank Lloyd Wright's Prairie style, has lots of kids' fare, finished with a root-beer float or a sundae in a waffle-cone bowl. The **Northbrook Court Shopping Center food court** (2171 Lake Cook Rd., Northbrook, tel. 847/498–1770) has the usual.

SCULPTURE ALFRESCO WALKING TOUR

When the Daley Civic Center was finished in 1965, a Chicago architect looked at the big, empty plaza in front and knew what it needed: a sculpture by the great artist Pablo Picasso. But when the unnamed, 50-foot-tall, 162-ton, rust-color steel figure was unveiled in 1967, Chicagoans were stunned. What was it, they wondered? The artist said it was a woman's head with flowing hair. Others thought it resembled an Afghan dog, butterfly, or eagle. One politician suggested it be replaced by a monument to Cubs player Ernie Banks. Eventually the brouhaha died down. Chicagoans began calling the sculpture "The Picasso," and modern art became accepted in the city landscape. In fact, if one piece was good, more would be better, and Chicago began amassing an impressive collection of public art by renowned modern artists. To inspire young Tinker Toy tinkerers, take a self-guided tour along Dearborn Street, from Jackson to Randolph streets, with short detours down side streets to the west.

Though known more for mobiles, Alexander Calder created a stabile called *Flamingo* (Federal Plaza, Adams and Dearborn Sts.), with big red steel arches. Marc Chagall used stone chips

EATS FOR KIDS Marshall Field's (111 N. State St., tel. 312/781–1000) has two good lunch places on the seventh floor. The **Walnut Room,** especially popular with families at Christmastime, is the more elegant, while **7 on State** is the more casual. **The Village** (71 W. Monroe St., tel. 312/332–7005) serves Italian food in a dining room decorated to look like an Italian town. Semi-private booths resemble buildings, such as a convent, a bank, and a prison, and there are lots of little twinkling lights. Kids can order half portions of pasta or have pizza or meatball sandwiches.

The Loop

 Free

312/744-2400 Chicago Office of
Tourism; www.cityofchicago.org

Daily sunrise–sunset

6 and up

and glass fragments in 250 colors in the mosaic *The Four Seasons* (First National Bank Plaza, Monroe and Dearborn Sts.). He even included bits of Chicago brick to depict the city at different times of the year and life at different stages. Louise Nevelson's *Dawn Shadows* (Wells and Madison Sts.) is a 30-foot-tall abstract piece inspired by the L train. Joan Miro's sculpture is aptly called *Miro's Chicago* (69 W. Washington St.). Some people think that this simple concrete figure of a woman with bright ceramic tiles on her skirt looks like a great Earth mother.

HEY, KIDS! How did you like the sculpture? What was your favorite? Imagine if you were a famous artist who was asked to make an outdoor sculpture for Chicago. What would it look like?

"The Picasso" (Dearborn and Washington Sts.) is still a bold symbol of Chicago. Its plaza has weekday noontime performances and a Christmas tree during the holidays (call 312/FINEART). Jean Dubuffet transformed doodles into the 29-foot-tall *Monument with Standing Beast* (James R. Thompson Center, 100 W. Randolph St.). One critic called it "the thinking man's Disneyland." Frankly, all these sculptures are like a roller coaster for the mind.

KEEP IN MIND Look for other modern outdoor sculptures around the city. Older public artworks depicting heroes and heroines and important events from Chicago's history can be found in the city's parks and on its buildings and bridges, so have your children keep an eye out for them everywhere. Take the time to read their plaques, which contain tidbits about the city's history and the people who made Chicago great.

SEARS TOWER SKYDECK

8

Like the Hancock Center, which predated it by three years, the 1,450-foot Sears Tower (1973) was the tallest building in the world for a while, until the spire-topped Petronas Towers were built in Kuala Lumpur, Malaysia, in 1996. Not surprisingly, its Skydeck provides a spectacular view of Chicago.

Pause in the waiting area to look at the model of Chicago (a preview of things to come) and a video about city and tower history. Next, board the elevator to the Skydeck, but hold onto your ears and stomach, as the elevator travels at 1,600 feet per minute. During the ascent, you'll see views of the city on a large screen. You may even think the elevator has overshot its mark as views from outer space appear. Never fear, you'll make a soft landing at the Skydeck, on the 103rd floor. On a clear day, four states are visible from the observation deck: Indiana, Michigan, Wisconsin, and, of course, Illinois, as well as the beautiful blue expanse of Lake Michigan. But your children might begin to wonder whether the elevator magically transported you all into a new Rick Moranis movie—*Honey, I*

HEY, KIDS!

Here's some tantalizing tower trivia: The last beam was signed by 12,000 construction workers, Sears employees, and other Chicagoans. At 76,000 tons, the building's steel frame is practically windproof; don't worry if it sways a bit. And don't worry about window washers, either. Robots clean the 16,000-plus windows.

EATS FOR KIDS On weekdays, you can try the Sears Tower's **Dos Hermanos** (tel. 312/993–0527), for Mexican food; the Italian **Mia Torre** (tel. 312/474–1350); or **Mrs. Levy's Deli** (tel. 312/993–0530) and her irresistible ice cream. (These are reached via a different lobby.) Open on weekdays *and* weekends, the large, bustling **Greek Islands** (200 S. Halsted St., tel. 312/782–9855) carries gyros as well as chicken, for the less adventurous. Kids are amazed by the flaming cheese dish called *saganaki*.

 233 S. Wacker Dr.; entrance on Jackson Blvd. between S. Wacker Dr. and Franklin St.

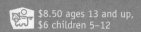 $8.50 ages 13 and up, $6 children 5–12

 Daily 9–11

312/975-9696; www.the-skydeck.com

 All ages

Shrunk Chicago—as everything is so far below that it looks miniature. Help them try to locate familiar landmarks, such as the United Center (where the Bulls play), various museums, and Chicago's third-tallest building, the John Hancock Center. Looking through a telescope is likely to reveal even more recognizable places—maybe even your own neighborhood.

An extensive renovation in 2000 created the Sights and Soul of Chicago, with exhibits revealing the movers and shakers, athletes, and artists who put Chicago back on the world map after the Great Fire of 1871. Knee-High Chicago, a series of dioramas from a four-foot-high perspective, give a kid's-eye view of the city. Children can peek through windows to see a model of the world's first Ferris wheel, part of the 1893 Columbian Exposition, or keep their cool while pretending to be a White Sox catcher as a baseball appears to whiz towards them. The aim is to add an eye-opening learning experience to the eye-popping view.

KEEP IN MIND At least 8,000 people visit the Skydeck daily, so expect to wait for up to an hour on a busy day. The midday hours (11–3) are the busiest, as are Monday and Friday, so to avoid crowds, go Tuesday–Thursday. For two views for the price of one, arrive just before dusk so you can see the city in daylight; watch the sunset, which can be spectacular; and stay for Chicago after dark, when twinkling lights transform it into a wonderland. It's not a problem; you can stay "on top" of Chicago as long as you want.

SIX FLAGS GREAT AMERICA

Daredevils and fraidy cats can both have fun here. Risk-takers find the screams and heart palpitations they're seeking on the Vertical Velocity (V2) roller coaster, which reaches 70 mph in less than four seconds as it shoots up a 185-foot spiral tower, or the Déjà Vu, which plummets almost straight down forward and then sends you through some loops before taking you on the same trip going backward. No wonder they're called mega- or hyper-coasters. Other giants include ShockWave, with seven loops; the Viper, reaching 100 feet; the American Eagle, at 127 feet; and Raging Bull, which plunges down 65 feet into a tunnel at more than 70 mph. The 1992 Batman coaster seems like child's play by comparison, but it's worth a ride for nostalgia's sake or for coaster-kids-in-training. For another adrenaline rush, try Splashwater Falls, where (surprise, surprise) boats plunge into water. Everyone gets wet, but that's the point. In warm weather, you dry off fast.

Younger kids head to kinder, gentler rides. The double-decker carousel is awesome, but your children might have trouble deciding which of the 88 horses and 15 other mounts to ride.

KEEP IN MIND If you're going with multiple children, take multiple adults in case one child wants you to go on a ride but another won't go along. Explain height restrictions beforehand, so kids are prepared for disappointment. Point out security officers, hosts, and hostesses, so your kids know whom to look for if they (or you) get lost, and familiarize yourself with the location of the Lost Parents station in the Hometown Park. Don't forget sunscreen, but travel light or store your belongings in lockers. And take snack breaks or entertainment breaks so no one gets to the breaking point.

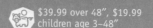
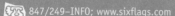

They'll feel right at home in Looney Tunes National Park, where they'll be greeted by old friends Bugs Bunny, Daffy Duck, and Taz and find a net climb and a train ride around cartoon land. Scooby Doo and the Flintstones hang out in Camp Cartoon Network. Little kids can feel grown-up when they ride Spacely's Sprocket Rockets, their own roller coaster. Another favorite, Sky Trek Tower takes youngsters calmly up 285 feet to look down on the whole "tiny" park.

There are also opportunities to sit still and be entertained, great when you're tired of nonstop action. Russian circus artists perform breathtaking feats, and magicians create spectacular illusions. You can also just stop and listen to a mariachi band or some rock and roll. For a more high-powered experience, take in an IMAX film, sometimes in 3-D; the theater's seats are synchronized to move with the action on screen. In fact, throughout the park you'll see a lot of action while sitting down.

HEY, KIDS! If you think you've done everything there is to do here, ask your parents to come during October Fright Fest—that is, if you think you won't be scared. The park is decorated for Halloween, and you're sure to encounter all sorts of creepy "people."

EATS FOR KIDS There is no lack of choices. You can sit down and have fried chicken or buffet-style turkey and roast beef or stick with the simple stuff like pizzas, hot dogs, and tacos. Options include **Angelo's Pasta and Pizza,** in Yankee Harbor; **Crazy Buffalo Saloon,** a sit-down restaurant in Southwest Territory; and **Aunt Martha's,** which serves chicken in Hometown Square.

SKOKIE NORTHSHORE SCULPTURE PARK

6

Art in the park reaches monumental proportions at this outdoor display, where 60 contemporary sculptures are spread out over 2 miles. Amazingly, they don't stand out awkwardly from their environment but rather blend into this prairie landscape shaded by beautiful old trees. Even more amazing, there's not a DO NOT TOUCH sign to be seen, and youngsters can discover the joys of exploring art hands-on—literally (climbing on the artworks is a no-no, though).

The subject matter of some of the sculptures will be obvious, even to very young children. *Charger I* and *Charger II* are two brightly painted steel horses. *Immigrant Gate* has a door of opportunity that can be pushed open. *Apple Rocket* is just that, an apple with a rocket where the stem should be. *A World of Difference,* in the Young Artists section, depicts the diversity of the students in the high school of the young people who created the work. Others are more abstract, providing endless opportunities for your children to use their imaginations, guessing at the artworks' meaning and seeing all sorts of objects within

EATS FOR KIDS Local favorite **Herm's Palace** (3406 Dempster St., tel. 847/673–9757) has hot dogs, char-burgers, gyros, nachos, and cheese fries as well as video games, some on the violent side. **Leona's** (3517 Dempster St., tel. 847/982–0101) serves pizza, traditional Italian food, and chicken fingers.

HEY, KIDS! If you're like most kids, your favorite sculpture will be the bright-colored *New Hope Risin'*. Be sure to check it out. It's near the parking lot, halfway between the Dempster Street and Main Street sections of the park. Made of various recycled objects, it contains numerous whirligigs spinning in the wind. Look closely at its many elements. You might even be inspired to go home, find some recyclables, and make your own sculpture. But do your parents a favor: Make yours smaller.

 East side of McCormick Blvd. between
Dempster St. and Touhy Ave., Skokie

 Free

 Daily sunrise–sunset

847/583-8549;
www.sculpturepark.org

 All ages

them. Only 25% of the sculptures are permanent, however; the rest are on loan and may eventually
be replaced.

As for how best to enjoy the park, you have a few choices. Some families take a stroll, stopping
at sculptures along the way. Others—mostly local Skokie and Evanston families who tend
to pedal leisurely—take to the bike path that runs through the sculpture park, bordered
on one side by whizzing cars and on the other by an idyllic tree-lined canal, where fish
can occasionally be seen jumping out of the water. But there's no hubbub here. Even though
a major thoroughfare runs along one side of this outdoor museum, the park is wide enough
so that it's easy to ignore the traffic. The setting is tranquil and free of crowds, but it's
not a whispering, tiptoeing, art museum kind of quiet. Grassy areas invite children to
romp, while shady spaces call parents to sit and rest. As in children's lives, art and
play flow together.

KEEP IN MIND There is a lot for children to see and absorb here,
and your kids will probably want to do a fair amount of just plain roaming,
too. To make a visit even more enlightening, check out the Web site's 26-page
self-guided tour. You might want to break up your visit into two parts, with
lunch sandwiched in between. Or even split your exploration into two separate trips. Making this easy is on-site parking at both the north and south sections: in the center of the Dempster Street to Main Street area and in the Howard
Street to Touhy Avenue stretch.

SPORTS PARK

At these two miniature courses, golf is more than just a sport with winners and losers and keeping score.

While playing the 18 holes of Traveler's Quest, older children can not only perfect their putting skills, but they can also take an imaginary trip around the world. The first hole is "home base"—a group of buildings including two of Chicago's tallest skyscrapers: the John Hancock Center and Sears Tower. Never fear; these are pint-size replicas. The global journey includes a stop at an African watering hole, where kids have to hit the ball through a hole in a hippo's open mouth, and a trip to Paris to putt under the Eiffel Tower. The best bet for a morale-boosting hole-in-one is at the Maya Temple, which is a straight shot on a flat surface. The most difficult feat is at the uphill Great Wall of China, but the effort required

HEY, KIDS! Do you know how many continents appear in Traveler's Quest? All seven: Africa, Antarctica, Asia, Australia, Europe, North America, and South America. Look for frigid Antarctica's representative (penguins) or the Australian native: a koala hiding in a tree. How about a walk on the Great Wall of China? It might take a while. It's 4,500 miles long. If you're not afraid of heights, you can go to Paris to climb the Eiffel Tower or just stay home and visit Chicago's Hancock Observatory and Sears Tower Skydeck (see #42 and #8). The ones here may look tall, but wait 'til you see the real ones.

3459 Oakton St., Skokie

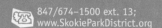
847/674–1500 ext. 13;
www.SkokieParkDistrict.org

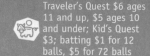
Traveler's Quest $6 ages
11 and up, $5 ages 10
and under; Kid's Quest
$3; batting $1 for 12
balls, $5 for 72 balls

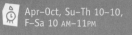
Apr–Oct, Su–Th 10–10,
F–Sa 10 AM–11PM

3 and up

is nothing compared to what it took to build the ancient wall itself. Read the labels at each hole to find out more about all the landmarks and locations.

Though children of any age are allowed to play Traveler's Quest, the nine-hole Kid's Quest is specifically for preschoolers. These fun-loving youngsters can putt and play to their heart's content on a layout that's part miniature golf course and part playground. Yes, little ones might actually succeed in hitting the ball into the hole, but they will be just as pleased to climb into a jeep parked at one of the holes, follow their ball through a tunnel, or watch it carried along by a waterfall and dropped onto the putting green. Kids will have a ball and adults will, too.

KEEP IN MIND
The Sports Park also has batting cages that launch softballs and baseballs whizzing toward the batter at various speeds. This is a place for kids who have some experience hitting a ball, not one for beginners to get their first lesson.

EATS FOR KIDS The Sports Park has a **concession stand** that has the usual hot dogs, nachos, soft drinks, and sweets. For more choices, see the Skokie Northshore Sculpture Park.

SPRING VALLEY NATURE CENTER
AND VOLKENING HERITAGE FARM

Take a walk back in time through a prairie of 6-foot-tall grasses and wildflowers—much like the beautiful but intimidating landscape that pioneers encountered—and then through marsh and woodland, on your way to an 1880s farmhouse and barn. It's here that your family can learn about the life of early settlers.

On weekends volunteers in period clothes are busy cooking and doing laundry, cleaning the barn, and feeding the animals. There are plenty of hungry mouths waiting: chickens, turkeys, hogs, and draft horses. There are also cows to be milked and sheep to be sheared in the spring, and helping hands are always needed. You may have trouble getting your children to clean their rooms or do laundry at home, but here they'll probably pitch right in, pumping water into a bucket to wash clothes, carrying wood for the stove, picking herbs in the garden, and even cleaning out the animal stalls.

Kids will discover how time-consuming chores used to be. Time for fun was short, and

KEEP IN MIND Check out the two gardens outside the visitor center. They'll give you ideas of native plants, fruits, and vegetables that you and your children can plant in your own backyard.

EATS FOR KIDS To have a meal in a completely different environment, travel to the Woodfield Mall (Rtes. 53 and 58), where you can visit a tropical jungle at the **Rainforest Café** (tel. 847/619–1900) or outer space at **Mars 2112** (tel. 847/885–2112), which serves familiar fare with out-of-this-world names. Perhaps your kids want the Roswell pizza, the crater burger, or one of the Soft Landings (desserts). If you just want quick, American fast food, the mall has that, too.

 1111 E. Schaumburg Rd., Schaumburg

 Free

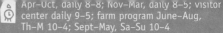 Apr–Oct, daily 8–8; Nov–Mar, daily 8–5; visitor center daily 9–5; farm program June–Aug, Th–M 10–4; Sept–May, Sa–Su 10–4

 847/985-2100

5 and up

without CDs and VCRs, entertainment consisted of singing along with the pump organ in the farmhouse's living room and looking at 3-D pictures of faraway places in the stereopticon, a distant ancestor of the View-Master and IMAX movies. Kids can also learn how to make cloth bunnies, twisted caterpillars, and other old-fashioned crafts on Sundays 1–4 in the farm's cabin.

There's other work to be done during annual festivals. At the Sugar Bush Fair, in March, kids see how maple syrup is made. During the Backyards for Nature Fair, they can make a birdhouse and plant a prairie flower to take home. At June's Mowing and Mooing, they can learn how to make butter, cheese, and ice cream, and during the Autumn Harvest Festival, in October, they can help with the harvest, milk the cow, and squeeze apple cider. If they're exhausted after so much effort, you can ride back to the visitor center in a wagon pulled by an old-time tractor. It may be bumpy, but it's easier than walking.

HEY, KIDS! You may see animals outside along the trail, but you're sure to see them in the visitor center, which has turtles, bullfrogs, and a bee-hive with a hole in the wall so the bees can go outside. You can also borrow binoculars and go outdoors for some bird-watching.

SWEDISH AMERICAN MUSEUM CENTER

I n 1976 the King of Sweden came to Chicago for the inauguration of the Swedish American Museum Center, celebrating the history and culture of Sweden and Swedish immigrants in the United States. Fittingly, the center is in Andersonville, an area on the city's north side where many of those immigrants settled.

Though the first floor offers a changing array of arts and crafts exhibitions and the second has a do-not-touch display of artworks and artifacts depicting the lives of Swedish immigrants, the third floor has been transformed into the Children's Museum of Immigration. Kids feel right at home here as they experience firsthand the hardships on a small 19th-century Swedish farm and the dream of making a better life in the New World. Children can milk a miniature cow (not easy), gather wood for the stove, and make a frugal make-believe meal of fish, potatoes, and eggs in a well-furnished farmhouse. If they undo the swaddling around a baby doll, they'll discover a coin on its belly button—to keep evil spirits away.

KEEP IN MIND Although the museum focuses on Swedish immigrants in America, their experiences are similar to those of people from other countries. So why not use your visit to talk to your children about their heritage and how it's part of your lives?

EATS FOR KIDS For a culinary trip to Sweden stop at **Ann Sather's** (5207 N. Clark St., tel. 773/271–6677), where kids love the thin Swedish pancakes served with tart red lingonberries. Everyone loves the homemade cinnamon rolls slathered with frosting. **Svea** (5236 N. Clark St., tel. 773/275–7738), a homey, diner-style storefront with a few tables, has Swedish pancakes, too. The **Swedish Bakery** (5348 N. Clark St., tel. 773/561–8919) sells butter cookies and bright-colored marzipan (almond paste) animals. Because Andersonville is now multiethnic, you can also get chicken shish kebab and other Middle Eastern dishes at **Reza's** (5255 N. Clark St., 773/561–1898).

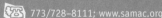 5211 N. Clark St.

 $4 adults, $3 children 3–18 and students

T–F 1–4, Sa–Su 10–3

773/728–8111; www.samac.org

3–12

Good luck was definitely needed for the grueling trip across the ocean. Your kids can board a large replica of a steamship to relive the voyage. At journey's end, they can enter a big log cabin, like the ones Swedes introduced in their new homeland. It may be sparsely furnished, but it was home sweet home.

Some Swedish-Americans kept on traveling. Murals depict Charles Lindbergh making the first transatlantic airplane flight and astronaut Buzz Aldrin landing on the moon. There is also a graphic reminder of the plight of immigrants today: an authentic raft used by people fleeing oppression in their homeland. Ask your children if they know about any immigrants that have been in the news.

The museum holds an outdoor Midsommarfest (second week of June), a Festival of Lights in honor of Santa Lucia (second week in December), and several parties inspired by literary character Pippi Longstocking, the strongest girl in the world.

HEY, KIDS! Peek into the tree stump in the Swedish farmyard. You can see the home of the imaginary Little People. Swedes believed that the Little People lived in tree trunks or under the floors in houses and that they could cast good or evil spells. Do you know any characters in books or movies who can cast spells?

TERRA MUSEUM OF AMERICAN ART

American artists such as Mary Cassatt, Winslow Homer, Edward Hopper, Georgia O'Keeffe, and James Whistler grab the spotlight at this museum, whose permanent collection is the result of one man's passion. The late Daniel Terra, an ambassador-at-large for cultural affairs under Ronald Reagan, acquired many works by American artists and then created this museum to display them.

To avoid a helter-skelter approach, ask for a free "Family Guide," available for each of the changing exhibitions. Guides are full of questions and activities that will slow children down and encourage them to look closely at the art. Your kids can read about how a curator decides on the main idea of an exhibition and then makes it a reality or learn how to decipher the labels for the works on the gallery walls. Guides also give suggestions of what to look for in paintings, such as the clues in *Painting No. 50,* a dreamlike vision by Marsden Hartley, that reveal the artist's interest in Native American culture. Or kids might

EATS FOR KIDS The **Corner Bakery** (676 N. St. Clair St., tel. 312/266–2570) has sandwiches and pizzas. At **Coco Pazzo Cafe** (636 N. St. Clair St., tel., 312/664–2777), adults enjoy Tuscan dishes while children order simple pastas or breaded chicken fingers with fries. And there's an artistic bonus: murals depicting Modigliani-style portraits. For a taste of Chicago history, eat at **Pizzeria Uno** (29 E. Ohio St., tel. 312/321–1000), where deep-dish pizza was created in 1943. It's very filling as well as popular, so waits can be long. The pizza at its nearby relative, **Pizzeria Due** (619 N. Wabash Ave., 312/943–2400), is exactly the same.

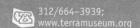 664 N. Michigan Ave.

 $7, T and 1st Su of mth free

T 10–8, W–Sa 10–6, Su 12–5

312/664-3939;
www.terramuseum.org

5 and up

be asked to look at the colors and brush strokes in a still life called *Strawberries*, by William J. McCloskey. Kids can become artists, too, because the guides include space for them to create their own masterpieces. (Pencils only, please, as an errant pen mark could harm the art.)

Free Family Fare workshops, held the first Sunday of every month at 1, offer a more formal art education. Kids first get inspiration from works in the museum and then unleash their own creativity in studio time. After looking at seasonal scenes in the exhibit Art and Nature: Hudson River School, children got to create their own imaginary species in a three-dimensional environment. After a tour of an exhibit of prints, they created a relief print using a Styrofoam plate, ink, and artist's tools. It's a chance for youngsters to experience the joy of artistic expression.

KEEP IN MIND
The museum staff likes to let kids learn by choosing the works that interest them. Children might prefer one that depicts a child or a dog or even something abstract with bright colors. Ask open-ended questions to help your kids explore subject matter and technique.

HEY, KIDS! Take a ride in the museum's elevator, which is probably almost as big as your bedroom. Why do you think it's so big? It's not just so it can hold a lot of people. Look at the painting called *Gallery of the Louvre*, by Samuel F.B. Morse; it's about 6 feet tall and 9 feet wide. Now do you understand why the elevator is so spacious? Morse painted it in Paris and brought it to the United States, where he wanted to charge people admission to see it. Though his plan was unsuccessful, he was successful at something else. He developed Morse code.

THOMAS HUGHES CHILDREN'S LIBRARY

After the Great Chicago Fire destroyed most of the city in 1871, Thomas Hughes, a member of the British Parliament and the author of *Tom Brown's School Days,* solicited donations of books for the city. Many well-known authors, including Lewis Carroll, sent copies of their works, and the 8,000 volumes that were collected seeded what would become Chicago's main library, which in 1991 moved here. What's ironic is that, unbeknownst to Mr. Hughes, Chicago didn't even have a library before the fire. Nevertheless, it seems only fitting that the city's children's library should take its name from this optimistic, benevolent man.

The children's library is home to more than 100,000 volumes in a very family-friendly setting. There are plenty of child-size tables and chairs and a special reading area for toddlers and their parents. Your children won't have any trouble finding some of the best books in the collection, because Caldecott and Newbery award winners are shelved separately. Kids can request a list of recommended books organized by age, from preschool to eighth grade.

KEEP IN MIND Children can get their own library card as soon as they can print their full name. If your child is just learning to write, why not practice before coming? A parent or legal guardian must cosign and show identification with name and Chicago address.

HEY, KIDS! Look for more than 70 objects from children's literature in the Storybook Dollhouse. Some are from well-known books, poems, and nursery rhymes; others are more obscure. The peach from *James and the Giant Peach* isn't hard to find, nor is the top hat of the Mad Hatter that Alice encountered in Wonderland. Can you guess what book the silver shoes come from? You may be surprised. In the movie *The Wizard of Oz,* Dorothy wears ruby slippers, but in the book they're silver.

Harold Washington Library Center,
400 S. State St.

Free

M–Th 9–7, F–Sa 9–5, Su 1–5

312/747–4200; www.chicagopubliclibrary.org

2–14

A special fund established NatureConnections, a collection of books, magazines, and videos about natural history, including dinosaurs, of course. A Learning Center has Internet access and interactive multimedia computers with educational software. A Program Room is the site of free special activities on Saturday, including author readings and book signings, jugglers, magicians, and concerts. Toddler story times, for children as young as 24 months, include storytelling, puppetry, music, movement, and a craft; they're offered once a week for six weeks. One-hour Storytime Extravaganzas, for ages 3–5 and 6–8, are scheduled each month. In addition, the fund that established the NatureConnections book collection also funds occasional programs about natural history, usually held Saturday afternoons. Workshops range from making terrariums and bird feeders to presentations by Lincoln Park Zoo staff, who bring in small mammals and reptiles. The library also has a summer reading program with a different theme each year. You don't have to travel very far to find a world full of adventure at the library.

EATS FOR KIDS The library's **Beyond Words Cafe** (tel. 312/747–4680) serves both a cold and hot buffet, Monday–Saturday 11–3. In addition, children can choose soup and half a sandwich or a bagel with cream cheese. The **Berghoff** (17 W. Adams St., tel. 312/427–3170) is more than 100 years old, so it's worth seeing for history's sake. Its menu offers a lot of German classics and some American ones, too. For more options, such as deep-dish pizza at **Edwardo's,** *see* Chicago Playworks.

CLASSIC GAMES

"I SEE SOMETHING YOU DON'T SEE AND IT IS BLUE." Stuck for a way to get your youngsters to settle down in a museum? Sit them down on a bench in the middle of a room and play this vintage favorite. The leader gives just one clue—the color—and everybody guesses away.

"I'M GOING TO THE GROCERY..." The first player begins, "I'm going to the grocery and I'm going to buy..." and finishes the sentence with the name of an object, found in grocery stores, that begins with the letter "A." The second player repeats what the first player has said, and adds the name of another item that starts with "B." The third player repeats everything that has been said so far and adds something that begins with "C" and so on through the alphabet. Anyone who skips or misremembers an item is out (or decide up front that you'll give hints to all who need 'em). You can modify the theme depending on where you're going that day, as "I'm going to X and I'm going to see..."

FAMILY ARK Noah had his ark—here's your chance to build your own. It's easy: Just start naming animals and work your way through the alphabet, from antelope to zebra.

PLAY WHILE YOU WAIT

NOT THE GOOFY GAME Have one child name a category. (Some ideas: first names, last names, animals, countries, friends, feelings, foods, hot or cold things, clothing.) Then take turns naming things that fall into that category. You're out if you name something that doesn't belong in the category—or if you can't think of another item to name. When only one person remains, start again. Choose categories depending on where you're going or where you've been—historic topics if you've seen a historic sight, animal topics before or after the zoo, upside-down things if you've been to the circus, and so on. Make the game harder by choosing category items in A-B-C order.

DRUTHERS How do your kids really feel about things? Just ask. "Would you rather eat worms or hamburgers? Hamburgers or candy?" Choose serious and silly topics—and have fun!

BUILD A STORY "Once upon a time there lived..." Finish the sentence and ask the rest of your family, one at a time, to add another sentence or two. Bring a tape recorder along to record the narrative—and you can enjoy your creation again and again.

GOOD TIMES GALORE

WIGGLE & GIGGLE Give your kids a chance to stick out their tongues at you. Start by making a face, then have the next person imitate you and add a gesture of his own—snapping fingers, winking, clapping, sneezing, or the like. The next person mimics the first two and adds a third gesture, and so on.

JUNIOR OPERA During a designated period of time, have your kids sing everything they want to say.

THE QUIET GAME Need a good giggle—or a moment of calm to figure out your route? The driver sets a time limit and everybody must be silent. The last person to make a sound wins.

HIGH FIVES

BEST IN TOWN
Brookfield Zoo
Chicago Children's Museum
Chicago Playworks
Field Museum of Natural History
North Avenue Beach

BEST OUTDOORS
Spring Valley Nature Center and Volkening Heritage Farm

WACKIEST
Eli's Cheesecake World

CULTURAL ACTIVITY
Art Institute of Chicago

NEW & NOTEWORTHY
Millennium Park

MUSEUM
DuPage Children's Museum

SOMETHING FOR EVERYONE

AMERICAN HISTORY
Bronzeville Children's Museum, **65**
Chicago Historical Society, **58**
DuSable Museum of African American History, **51**
Frank Lloyd Wright Home and Studio, **46**
The Grove, **43**
Peace Museum, **15**
Spring Valley Sanctuary and Volkening Heritage Farm, **4**

ANCIENT HISTORY
Field Museum of Natural History, **47**
Oriental Institute Museum, **16**
Rosenbaum ARTiFACT Center, **11**

ART ATTACK
Art Institute of Chicago, **66**
Chicago Cultural Center, **59**
DuSable Museum of African American History, **51**
Frank Lloyd Wright Home and Studio, **46**
Mexican Fine Arts Center Museum, **28**
Museum of Contemporary Art, **24**

Sculpture Alfresco Walking Tour, **9**
Skokie Northshore Sculpture Park, **6**
Terra Museum of American Art, **2**

COOL 'HOODS
The L, **34**
Mexican Fine Arts Center Museum, **28**
New Maxwell Street Market, **20**
Sculpture Alfresco Walking Tour, **9**

CULTURE CLUB
Bronzeville Children's Museum, **65**
DuSable Museum of African American History, **51**
Mexican Fine Arts Center Museum, **28**
Mitchell Museum of the American Indian, **26**
Oriental Institute Museum, **16**
Swedish American Museum Center, **3**

FARMS AND ANIMALS
Brookfield Zoo, **64**
The Grove, **43**
Indian Boundary Park, **38**

John G. Shedd Aquarium, **36**
Lincoln Park Zoo, **29**
Peggy Notebaert Nature Museum, **13**
Ryerson Woods, **10**
Spring Valley Nature Sanctuary and Volkening Heritage Farm, **4**

FOOD FIXATION
Eli's Cheesecake World, **50**
Spring Valley Nature Sanctuary and Volkening Heritage Farm, **4**

FREEBIES
Chicago Mercantile Exchange, **57**
Chicago Music Mart at DePaul Center, **56**
Navy Pier, **21**
New Maxwell Street Market, **20**
Peace Museum, **15**
Pedway, **14**
Thomas Hughes Children's Library, **1**

GAMES AND AMUSEMENTS
ESPN Zone, **48**
Six Flags Great America, **7**

GOOD SPORTS
Chicago White Sox, **54**
ESPN Zone, **48**
Lakefront Bike Way, **33**
Lattof YMCA, **32**
Millennium Park, **27**
North Avenue Beach, **19**
North Branch Bicycle Trail, **18**
Sports Park, **5**

LOST IN SPACE
Adler Planetarium and Astronomy Museum, **68**
Six Flags Great America, **7**

ON THE WILD SIDE
Caldwell Woods, **62**
North Branch Bicycle Trail, **18**
North Park Village Nature Center, **17**
Ryerson Woods, **10**
Spring Valley Nature Sanctuary and Volkening Heritage Farm, **4**

PARKS AND GARDENS
Chicago Botanic Garden, **61**
Garfield Park Conservatory, **45**
Harold Washington Playlot Park, **41**
Indian Boundary Park, **38**
Lakefront Bike Way, **33**
Millennium Park, **27**
Skokie Northshore Sculpture Park, **6**

PLANES, TRAINS, AND AUTOMOBILES
Illinois Railway Museum, **39**
Museum of Science and Industry, **22**

RAINY DAYS
Chicago Children's Museum, **60**
DuPage Children's Museum, **52**
Garfield Park Conservatory, **45**
Kohl Children's Museum, **35**
Lattof YMCA, **32**
Pedway, **14**
Peggy Notebaert Nature Museum, **13**
Thomas Hughes Children's Library, **1**

SCIENTIFIC TERRIFIC
Adler Planetarium and Astronomy Museum, **68**
Field Museum of Natural History, **47**
Health World, **40**
International Museum of Surgical Science, **37**
John G. Shedd Aquarium, **36**
Museum of Science and Industry, **22**

SHOW TIME
American Girl Place, **67**
Chicago Music Mart at DePaul Center, **56**
Chicago Playworks, **55**
Emerald City Theatre Company, **49**
Kohl Children's Museum, **35**
Let's Dress Up, **31**
Lifeline Theatre KidSeries, **30**
Museum of Broadcast Communications, **25**

TERRIFIC TOURS
Eli's Cheesecake World, **50**
The L, **34**
Sculpture Alfresco Walking Tour, **9**

TINIEST TOTS
Brookfield Zoo, **64**
Chicago Children's Museum, **60**
Diversey Miniature Golf, **53**
DuPage Children's Museum, **52**
Garfield Park Conservatory, **45**
Harold Washington Playlot Park, **41**
Kohl Children's Museum, **35**
Lincoln Park Zoo, **29**

TIRE THEM OUT
Chicago White Sox, **54**
ESPN Zone, **48**
Harold Washington Playlot Park, **41**
Lakefront Bike Way, **33**
Lattof YMCA, **32**
North Avenue Beach, **19**
North Branch Bicycle Trail, **18**
Rainbow Falls Water Park, **12**

WATER, WATER EVERYWHERE
Buccaneer Pirate Adventure Cruises, **63**
Caldwell Woods, **62**

Indian Boundary Park, **38**
North Avenue Beach, **19**
Rainbow Falls Water Park, **12**

WAY UP HIGH
Adler Planetarium and Astronomy Museum, **68**
Grosse Point Lighthouse, **44**
Hancock Observatory, **42**
Sears Tower Skydeck, **8**
Six Flags Great America, **7**

WEIRD AND WACKY
Buccaneer Pirate Adventure Cruises, **63**
Chicago Mercantile Exchange, **57**
Eli's Cheesecake World, **50**
International Museum of Surgical Science, **37**
The L, **34**
Let's Dress Up, **31**
Museum of Holography, **23**
Pedway, **14**

ALL AROUND TOWN

ALBANY PARK
North Park Village Nature Center, 17

ANDERSONVILLE
Swedish American Museum Center, 3

BRIDGEPORT
Chicago White Sox, 54

DOWNTOWN SOUTH
Rosenbaum ARTiFACT Center, 11
Sears Tower Skydeck, 8

HYDE PARK
DuSable Museum of African American History, 51
Harold Washington Playlot Park, 41
Museum of Science and Industry, 22
Oriental Institute Museum, 16

LINCOLN PARK
Chicago Historical Society, 58
Diversey Miniature Golf, 53
Emerald City Theatre Company, 49
Lincoln Park Zoo, 29
North Avenue Beach, 19

THE LOOP
Art Institute of Chicago, 66
Buccaneer Pirate Adventure Cruises, 63
Chicago Cultural Center, 59
Millennium Park, 27
Museum of Broadcast Communications, 25

NEAR NORTH
American Girl Place, 67
Chicago Children's Museum, 60
Hancock Observatory, 42
International Museum of Surgical Science, 37
The L, 34
Museum of Contemporary Art, 24
Navy Pier, 21
Terra Museum of American Art, 2

NEAR WEST
New Maxwell Street Market, 20

PILSEN
Mexican Fine Arts Center Museum, **28**

ROGERS PARK
Indian Boundary Park, **38**
Lifeline Theatre KidSeries, **30**

SOUTH LAKE SHORE DRIVE
Adler Planetarium and Astronomy Museum, **68**
Field Museum of Natural History, **47**
John G. Shedd Aquarium, **36**

SOUTH LOOP
Chicago Music Mart at DePaul Center, **56**
Chicago Playworks, **55**

STREETERVILLE
ESPN Zone, **48**

WEST LOOP
Chicago Mercantile Exchange, **57**
Museum of Holography, **23**

WEST SIDE
Garfield Park Conservatory, **45**

MANY THANKS

I would like to dedicate this book to my mother, who was always full of good ideas. When my sisters and I were growing up, she took us swimming, horseback riding, ice skating, and walking in the woods and on trips to the big city to see museums and zoos and Broadway plays. I owe my love of adventurous family outings to her. I am grateful to all the people in the Chicagoland area who have contributed information to this book for their belief that children are our most precious resource. Many thanks also to editor Andrea Lehman, the queen of the well-placed question mark and expert in family-friendly prose. I would like to thank my husband, Alain, who is such a good sport and great navigator in my constant search for new activities, and my sons, Stéphane and Theodore, who are specialists at "doing levers" at hands-on museums and are always an inspiration. Thanks for letting me be a child in the family, too.

—Nancy Maes